Rare disease: An extraordin[ary gift]

A journey with chronic disea[se]

Putting the words 'rare disease' and extraordinary gift' together in the same sentence may appear bizarre and even contradictory to most people. Once it would have done to me too, but like many others, my family have been on a strange journey where quite unexpectedly a rare disease invited itself into our lives. This unwanted adventure has been scary, lonely, desperate, heartbreaking and confusing. It has been educating, infuriating, enlightening, joyous and YES, especially extraordinary.

I know that some of you are on that journey right now and depending how far along it you are, you may be feeling any or all of the above descriptions. Even if this is not a journey that has come your way, you can learn from this book and be ready should you or anyone you love ever have to take it. It may not be a rare disease journey specifically, it may be any chronic illness or debilitating condition or just a life changing event that unexpectedly arrives and like a tsunami sweeps you and those around you away. However this story is about a rare disease called

Obliterative Bronchiolitis (OB) and how it changed our lives.

The arrival of a rare disease, like Obliterative Bronchiolitis unceremoniously dumps a whole truck load of unordered emotions including great sorrow and indescribable fear but it also brings something else quite wonderful and that is hope. Hope is unique to human beings and it is the one thing that cannot be taken away by someone else. It's personal and it belongs to you and it's up to you how you use it. Hope is the vessel that carries you through the terrifying journey from the land of despair and confusion into the strange new world of unimagined emotions, amazing people and incredible experiences that you had never imagined existed before. This book is the journey to the land of the 'extraordinary' and when you get there you will realise that you are extraordinary too.

Lynne ☺

OB is also known as Bronchiolitis Obliterans or BO in other parts of the world and will be referred to as this in parts of the book where applicable.

Chapter 1

The Unwanted Gift Arrives

People often say things like, 'you never know what's around the corner' or 'life sometimes throws you a curve ball'. You've probably flippantly said things like that yourself, I certainly had. I guess just like me, most people, don't really think about what that actually means and guess it will never really apply to them. After all bad things don't happen to good people do they?

Well I am going to share our story when we discovered that bad things do happen and right when you least expect them.

In 2004 I had a perfectly healthy beautiful eight year old daughter called Kiri. We had just come back from living in New Zealand and for the previous 7 years she had grown up running around under cloudless turquoise skies, on picture perfect beaches, it was an idyllic childhood. She was bursting with health and vitality and we were excited about our return to the UK to be close to family and friends again. We had a good life, nice home, lovely family and everything was set for a brilliant future, or so it seemed.

Four months later my lovely daughter simply 'caught a cold' and that was when our unwanted gift slipped quietly in.

Our GP failed to pick up the signs of danger, maybe because we were squeezed in for an emergency appointment late at night, maybe he was tired, or simply wanted to get home to his own family but for whatever reason despite all the very obvious signs before him he simply did <u>not</u> listen to her chest and we were sent home with paracetamol and a cursory pat on the head. That was the defining moment when our lives were about to change forever.

Twelve hours later she was being rushed to hospital, blue lights, sirens, and the whole terrifying drama began to unfold. The local hospital were unable to stabilize her and so seven hours later there was another ambulance ride to another larger hospital and before we could begin to process what was happening, she was in the paediatric intensive care unit wired up to beeping machines and drips and tubes. The 'simple cold' he had diagnosed had turned to pneumonia and that was the moment that the unknown virus sneaked in quietly and began all its terrible devastation. We still had no idea what was happening to our little girl, all we knew was that our baby was fighting for her life and we couldn't do anything to help her.

Anyone whose child has been in an intensive care unit will testify that it is a surreal experience. You are rendered completely and totally impotent, all the decisions surrounding your child are being made by others and all you can do is be a helpless bystander, terrified and numb. Up until that point you have been the one who has been totally in control of everything that happened your child, they have relied on you completely, they trust you to make everything right. You are their life line and then suddenly you are not; you are superfluous and just as lost as they are.

I have only the utmost admiration for the dedication and skill of doctors and nurses in PICU (Paediatric Intensive Care Unit). Here the seamless and devoted care was faultless. Although terrified and bemused by the events that were happening we felt our girl was in the best possible hands. A nurse sat constantly by her bedside and monitored her all the time, doctors seemed to be always at hand, the slightest change was noted and the reactions were swift and confident. It was reassuring though daunting.

Our daughter seemed to be shrinking by the minute, lost amongst tubes, masks, drips, and machines. The constants beeps and lights were confusing and frightening. What did it mean when that monitor beeped or light flashed? Every change threatened more danger. She seemed so fragile and tiny, and as she began to curl over in a foetal position we were terrified she might be leaving us and felt helpless to do anything to stop it.

There were only a few lucid moments of connection, the worst when she was put on a Bi-PaP machine. We were warned it is hard to watch when the mask is put on. As the huge mask swallowed her tiny face and they attached the bonnet to keep it in place, it seemed to smother her. Her eyes met mine and momentarily I witnessed the sheer terror and fear she was feeling, it was so acutely painful I had to turn away. I can still feel that excruciating moment. Fortunately she can't remember any of it. I am sure many other parents have had similar experiences with ventilation and oxygen support, several other parents have shared similar feelings with me and we will talk about oxygen dependence in greater depth later in the book.

A Bi-Level positive air pressure machine is a device which assists with breathing. It is connected by flexible tubing to a face mask worn by the patient. The Bi-PaP machine helps push air and oxygen into the lungs and helps to hold the lungs inflated, thereby allowing more oxygen to enter the lungs. A Bi-PaP machine is used when a patient cannot breathe effectively enough to maximize the transport of oxygen into their lungs and the blood and can be used instead of a ventilator. There is some debate whether the use of mechanical ventilation increases the risk of OB or whether it is simply an indicator of the severity of the disease. This is an area where more research is needed to see if measures could or should be taken to protect the lungs of vulnerable children.

'The use of mechanical ventilation, an important treatment for children in intensive care units, has apparently allowed severely ill children to survive who previously would have died before BO could be recognised. Mechanical ventilation is indispensable for the support of critically ill patients with respiratory insufficiency. Although our study found that mechanical ventilation was a significant risk factor for post infectious BO, our results do not indicate whether it causes injury to the lung that increases the risk for developing post infectious BO or whether it merely serves as an indicator of severity of illness˙ Further research is needed to clarify the relationship between mechanical ventilation and post infectious BO, and to study whether lung protective strategies are needed for this vulnerable population.

Colom A J, Teper A M, Vollmer W M. *et al* **Risk factors for the development of post- infectious bronchiolitis obliterans in children with bronchiolitis.** Thorax 2006. 61 (6) 503–506.

At the time we did not question whether this procedure held any risk factors for our daughter we just wanted something to help her breathe. Eventually after forty-eight hours with no sleep the nurse persuaded us to go and rest and she promised not to leave my daughters side. I trusted her. I don't think we did more than doze but sleeplessness was going to be something we soon got used to. After a few days Kiri seemed to be improving and the tubes and drips began to deplete in number and she was moved to HDU (High Dependency Unit), this was progress we thought, things must be getting better. The consultant from PICU reassured us that she would be fine and we believed him. He didn't know that the unwanted gift had now embedded itself nicely, was making itself at home and was not going to leave.

We spent over a week in HDU, where I sat, slept (or rather didn't sleep) on a hard chair by her bed day and night. Progress was slow although eventually we made it to a side room. Here at least I felt a little more in control of our space. We were becoming hospitalised though, exhausted and depressed. Living on fast food and sugary drinks, no sleep and slowly feeling more and more disempowered and unheard.

> "*Hospitalization is one of the most stressful events that children and adults can experience. Children and adults reactions to hospitalization, such as anxiety, fear, withdrawal, depression, regression and defiance, can be more severe than their reactions to the illness*" (Froehlich, 1984).

It's a strange phenomenon the way hospitalisation effects people, how quickly you can lose touch with reality of time on the 'outside' and how you can go into this experience as an assertive strong person and watch as your confidence disappears down the drain, it's a process of being made powerless. There are many challenges to face; the separation from family and friends, fear of the unfamiliar, uncertainty about hospital rules, loss of independence and identity, fear of pain and for many feeling they are just not able or allowed to question the consultants and doctors.

There have been many documented papers and books published on this subject that you can explore.

> **How to Survive Your Hospital Stay:** *The Complete Guide to Getting the Care You Need--And Avoiding Problems You Don't.* Lynn Sonberg Books
> **How to Survive Your Hospital Stay.** *Judy Burger Crane and Jason Young (June 1998)*
> **Confessions of a Professional Hospital Patient:** *A Humorous First Person Account of How to Survive a Hospital Stay. Michael A. Weiss (1 Feb 2001)*

Here are some of our tricks for survival ☺

You know your child best: Remember as 'the parent' you are still the **BEST** expert on your child. It's easy to feel intimated by all the medical jargon, the doctors talking about your child as if you are not in the room and the fact that decisions are being made without your input. Be strong and don't be afraid to have your say, you will be the one who notices the small changes in your child that the medical staff don't see. You know what is 'normal' for your child, you know best when your child is really sick.

If you're really not happy, SAY so and keep saying so: So many parents sit silently fuming with frustration or desperately unhappy because they feel they are not being listened to. I quickly learnt you just have to keep repeating yourself over and over until you get a response you are happy with. It's easier and quicker for staff to deal with parents who are compliant but if you are really uncomfortable about something you must say so; if for no other reason than the fact you are your child's champion. Imagine how scared they are and then if they see you crumbling and not able to fight their corner how much worse it becomes for them.

Give your child the power back: If it's bad enough for an adult in hospital imagine how terrifying it is for your child. They are hurting and ill and they don't understand why they feel like this. They are in an alien environment and they are listening to adults they don't even know who are talking about them with words they don't understand. Strange people are undressing them, prodding and poking them with needles and tubes and sometimes hurting them. Sometimes whole groups of strangers come all at once and surround them and as the child they can't just leave. Nobody asks their permission, or gives them a choice, they are powerless.

So give your child some power. Insist if the child is old enough that the medical staff talk to your child not talk over them, even toddlers are entitled to this consideration and respond to it. It makes them feel safer and less vulnerable

Try and let your child make some of the decisions, even if they only *think* they are making them. *'Would you like to have fun blowing bubbles?'* works much better than *'Stop playing now it's time for your physiotherapy'*, but has the same end result for their chest.

If something or some procedure is hurting your child and a nurse says something like *'don't be silly'* or worse *'no it isn't'* (we've had that one) insist they stop what they are doing immediately. You know your child, if they say it hurts, it hurts. You need to lead the way and show your child they are being heard and that their opinion counts. If not they are simply being made more helpless and afraid. I have had many a battle over waiting for sufficient time to allow numbing cream to work before injections because, *yes it does hurt otherwise*. Also making sure staff listen as my daughter really *does* know which vein works best for IV's and which one will never work so stop trying to get a needle in it! I am sure many on this journey have similar tales.

Just shift the power and you will all feel better.

During one particular hospital stay my daughter made a performance chart for the nurses. She hung it on the end of her bed with all her other charts. Every day she scored each nurse with smiley faces on how well they did certain things. Did they smile at her? Did they talk to her rather than me? Were they gentle with injections? It had an amazing effect. At first the nurses were quite 'put out' that a nine year old was scoring their behaviour but within a few days it became quite a competition. Each nurse wanted to have the most number of smiley faces on her shift, well why wouldn't they? The doctors began to look at the charts too. One asked why he wasn't given a score and so they were added to the chart as well. The effect on my daughter was amazing and it suddenly shifted the balance of power. She felt more in charge of what was happening to her and yes, guess what, she saw more smiling nurses, more nurses who took the time to talk to her and ensure she was comfortable.

Sometimes the simplest things make the biggest difference.

In the family survey carried out by Breathtakers OB Trust in 2010, 47% of families reported feeling intimidated and overruled by ward staff.

> 'Ward staff simply do not listen even when it is clear they have no idea about this condition. We often felt bullied by staff and as if we had no control over events unless we argued forcefully'
> Parent of a child with OB

Our story was now into its fourth week and the happy day finally came and we were discharged. We took home a very frail little girl, still coughing up green phlegm and looking very poorly and not eating. Doctors assured us it was fine, she would get stronger and get well. We were discharged without even a hospital follow up appointment. At this stage we just thought she had had pneumonia and the worst was over. Our unwelcome gift was still a secret though and unknown to us had now set up permanent residence.

FROM THE BESTSELLING AUTHOR OF

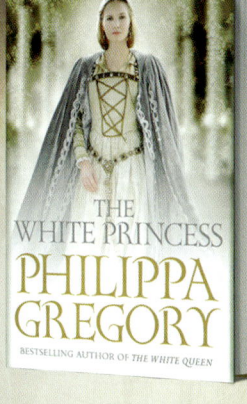

The White Queen

THE WHITE PRINCESS
PHILIPPA GREGORY

Philippa Gregory brings to vivid life the turbulent times of Elizabeth of York: Princess, outcast, lover, Queen

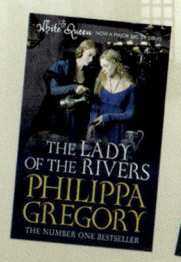

Available from all good booksellers
www.PHILIPPAGREGORY.com

Chapter 2

The diagnosis journey

The journey from 'acute illness' to a 'chronic disease' is a long, hard and desperate one for many families. Here is where the challenges may really begin, where you have to find strengths you never knew you had and face situations you never even knew existed. The good news is you will do all those things successfully and develop a new deeper understanding of life in the process, even if sometimes it feels like you are just drowning in the whole miserable process.

Once home again from hospital we wanted to believe that this had just been a horrible dream, all would be well now and simply go back to normal. It soon became very clear especially to me, that it just wasn't happening. Call it mothers' intuition, gut feeling or just knowing your child. I knew this just simply hadn't gone away and it was serious, but nobody seemed to want to listen to me.

For the next few months we went back and to the GP countless times, each time sent away with inhalers and nebulisers and the insistence she was fine. She had never made it back to school, she was still being sick every day; coughing endlessly through the night, breathless in the day. I was made to feel I was making it all up by medical staff, that I was a nuisance or worse a liar. I still kept going back.

I had given up work now. School was out of the question and I could see my child becoming more and more depressed and sick. I have heard this story repeated by so many families now over the last few years, it is depressingly familiar but no less shocking each time yet another distraught family relay it to me.

We had had two emergency hospital admissions to the local hospital and still medical staff had not instigated further investigations to explore what was really wrong. It was labeled as asthma or allergies but still no real tests or answers. On the second of these admissions a social worker suddenly appeared to talk to my daughter. I recall thinking how young she looked, about the same age as my eldest son. It quickly became clear the direction the questioning was going in. She wanted to know if anything was happening at home. Was anybody upsetting or hurting my daughter? Was my daughter afraid of anything? In her opinion as there appeared to be no medical diagnosis, this must be panic attacks, a psychological problem or worse some kind of abuse. At some point in the conversation I must have been getting very upset, I remember becoming furious, as she told me very coolly if I didn't be quiet and let my daughter answer I'd be asked to leave and I wouldn't be allowed back to the ward. I was terrified; could someone just do that? Could they remove me from my child? I realized then I had to get another opinion and fast. I felt both totally disempowered and terrified in an instant.

By sheer chance a lovely young doctor was on the ward at the same time and saw I was upset. I was still adamant something was very wrong and I wasn't going to stop saying it. He sat and chatted to me over coffee. He had looked at my daughter's notes and it rang alarm bells for him too, he could see she was not recovering as she should have done. Three months had passed since the pneumonia and he agreed she should have been getting better. He knew a Respiratory Consultant at Southampton Hospital that he thought very highly of and said he would refer us immediately.

Though I didn't know it then that was our lucky day, without that we may have been like many other families affected by this disease who I learned later wait years, sometimes as many as ten years, to get a correct diagnosis. All I can say to those people who are trapped in the nightmare pre-diagnosis stage is please please don't give up. Keep being a nuisance, keep on fighting for your child until you get an answer, because if you know deep down it isn't right, believe me, it isn't right. Trust your parental instinct.

Breathtakers Family Survey: findings about diagnosis

Misdiagnosis is a big area of worry for many families. The results of Breathtakers Family survey in 2010 showed that 43% of families had received a misdiagnosis, the most common being asthma.

Misdiagnosis is not just distressing but can lead to a deterioration in quality of life and have an impact on the overall condition and outcome of OB as it delays the effective and appropriate treatment and management. It may also lead to more unnecessary hospital admissions for children with OB, unnecessary testing and treatment and adds to the burden of stress and worry.

The survey also revealed that persistence by families was a key factor for referral to a specialist and some families felt they had to 'fight' to get a diagnosis. The whole process for some families was very traumatic and stressful. Shorter referral time to a specialist consultant seemed to be the key to getting an accurate diagnosis more quickly. The survey revealed inequality and variation across the UK and the Republic of Ireland in referral timeframes and levels of support at diagnosis.

Lack of information at the time of diagnosis was also a recurring theme with a lot of families. Many expressed feelings of isolation and anxiety at diagnosis time and were unclear how to get information or support. 36% of families reported that their consultant did not discuss a care plan at diagnosis or give any information about the disease. Delays in diagnosis resulted in multiple hospital stays and GP visits which were extremely stressful for families and a drain on NHS resources.

In retrospect I feel our diagnosis journey was short and relatively straight forward compared to so many other families and yet I know also how stressful, exhausting and destructive it was, so for those poor families who wait years for a correct diagnosis it must be soul destroying.

Here's what some families said in the 2010 Family Survey....

'It took months of various admissions to the local hospital before our daughter was referred to a specialist'. OB parent

'We never thought we would get an answer as to what was really wrong, as a family we felt destroyed' OB parent

'We lived more at hospital than home for years. It affected every part of our life, emotionally and financially. The stress was indescribable'. OB parent

Misdiagnosis is one of the most common medical errors and it can have dire consequences, leading to unnecessary or delayed treatments and physical and emotional suffering.

Getting a correct diagnosis gives families a framework to both work with and build a plan from; without it families can feel lost, alone and for many there is the feeling of being 'not believed'. Families trapped in limbo and waiting for diagnosis often experience an inability to move forward or make decisions.

There is a huge emotional burden attached to lack of diagnosis or misdiagnosis and many families (mothers especially) are made to feel guilty and attention seeking. Our survey revealed that GP's in particular are very dismissive and unfeeling with 'serial' visitors to their surgery.

'Our GP does not acknowledge my son's condition; I always have to remind him, he's quite dismissive.' Mother of OB child

> '*I was told by GP's I was a paranoid Mother, as my son was ill every week from 23 days old, they didn't trust my instinct*'.
> OB Mother

During the whole period whilst waiting for diagnosis there may be many hospital stays, invasive tests and travelling to different hospitals. Waiting for test results can be frustrating and then disappointing when they do not give definitive answers or lead to any real treatment. Parents sometimes blame themselves and try constantly to find answers to what seems an unsolvable puzzle, adding to the emotional stress. Relationships struggle and everyone is exhausted. Along with this comes a feeling of being out of control and a huge fear of the future which is unknown. As humans we are constantly searching to find logical solutions and explanations and the long road to diagnosis can seem overwhelming.

Here's the good news. You *will* almost certainly get there. Even if it's a long and convoluted journey there are things you can do to help you on the road and retain your sanity and sense of humour at the same time.

Survival tips

- Enjoy all the little things. Don't get so lost in the medical maze that you miss the ordinary milestones and joyful events with your child.

- Don't make the illness the centre of your universe or every day will be miserable for you and your child.

- Your child is still just a child who wants to have fun, so let them.

- Live for the moment, not for what may or may not be, you can't see the future, stop trying.

- Here's a tough one but you need to accept that this has happened to your child and you can't change it, but you can change how you respond to it. To help your child, help yourself first.

- Stop comparing your child to others. This journey is going to be a different one so celebrate it. Every child is different. Focus on the good stuff, the things they have achieved and the fun times.

- Try and talk to others who are on the same or similar journey and get strength from each other.

- Try not to spend all your time trying to solve the problem or worrying about things you don't know. Stop looking at the big picture, you don't know what that is, instead take each challenge one at a time, day by day. It's less overwhelming that way.

- It's OK to ask for help, cry or just be sad sometimes.

- Don't feel guilty about taking time out for yourself. It's OK to have fun and it's paramount to look after your own health.

- Remember doctors are human too and they don't always have the answer much as you want them to. They are probably frustrated too that they can't find an answer.

- Don't try and self diagnose by Internet surfing, you'll only find bad and inaccurate information and feel worse ☹

The road to diagnosis is paved with multiple hospital visits often to multiple specialists. It is costly, time consuming, confusing and frustrating. Your child may be referred to several different specialists, in several different departments. You may have to tell your 'story' many different times including symptoms, tests, medications. Communications between the different specialists is sometimes poor and not timely. You may be left feeling that nobody understands your child and that no progress is being made.

Whilst this whole process is emotional, stressful and frustrating it is worth hanging onto the fact that it is NECESSARY. Every wrong avenue explored brings you closer to a correct diagnosis; it is often a process of elimination to get to the right answer. Even if you do not have clear diagnosis your specialist can still offer support which is tailored to your child's needs.

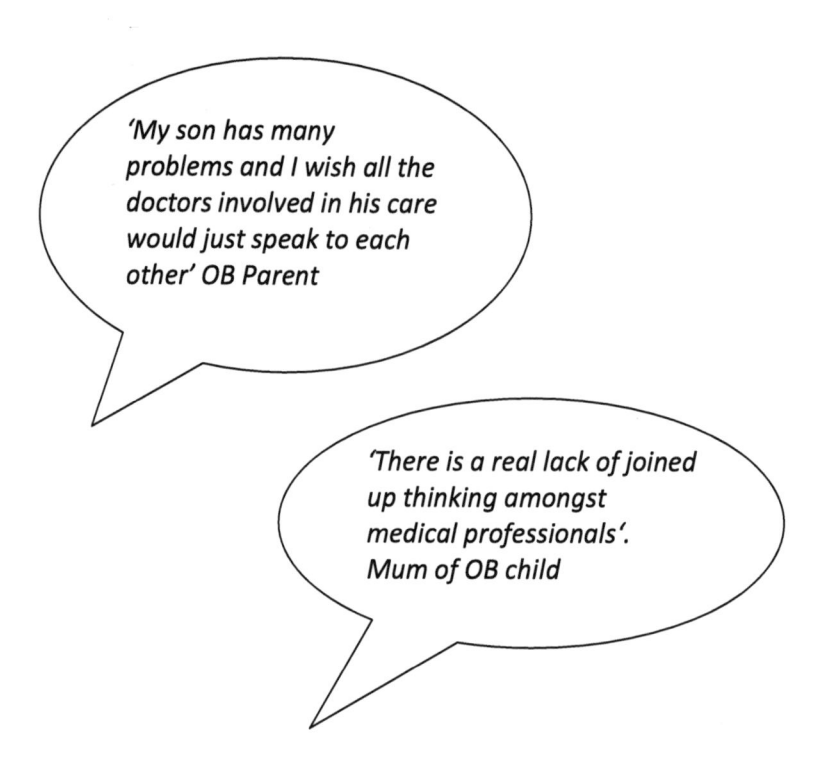

'My son has many problems and I wish all the doctors involved in his care would just speak to each other' OB Parent

'There is a real lack of joined up thinking amongst medical professionals'. Mum of OB child

Tips whilst waiting for diagnosis

- Keep a diary of all the appointments you go too and brief notes of what was said. As time passes it's impossible to remember who said what and when. Doctors will appreciate you doing this to as it helps to keep track of progress and makes appointments more focused and productive.

- You are still the best expert on your child; you will notice changes and milestones when nobody else does. Write them down and take the notes to every appointment. Put dates on everything you record. Keep a diary of your child's progress. This is also great to look back on and see what progress they have made.

- Take notes during an appointment, doctors will not think you are strange in fact they will encourage you to do this. If there are words or procedures you don't understand make a note of them and ask for an explanation. There is nothing worse than coming out of appointment even more confused than when you went in. It happens so many times to parents because they are afraid of looking silly and so don't ask questions.

- Make sure you receive all copies of letters and reports so that you are kept in the loop of events.

- Start a folder to keep all paperwork together and get in the habit of always using it. That way you won't be further frustrated by scrabbling around trying to find documents you know you have had but have misplaced.

- Develop a great relationship with your consultant's secretary because it is going to be long one, so ensure it's a good one ☺ They are always the most helpful and accessible person to call and the fast track route to your consultant.

- Make communication between GP's, consultants and everyone involved in your child's care YOUR responsibility. That way you can be sure it will get done and you won't get frustrated by other people's inefficiency.

- To cut down on the number of times you have to re-tell your story make a medical passport for your child. List key dates, symptoms, tests, significant illnesses, medications, likes or dislikes, and details of your GP and Consultant. Keep this updated and always carry with you to appointments. This is also great in emergencies.

- Every time you think of question, write it down on a memo pad and take along to your next appointment. This is great for your child too if they have questions. Often the actual appointment is overwhelming so if they have thought about it before they are more prepared.

- No question is a 'silly' question, so just ask it.

- Don't be afraid to ask for a second opinion if you are not satisfied. Any good doctor will not be offended by you asking for somebody else's opinion. If they do take umbrage all the more reason to get someone else involved.

- Having someone with you at appointments as a second pair of eyes and ears is great. It's surprising what we miss, especially when in an emotional state and its empowering for you to have support with you.

At the end of the day all you want are some answers that will enable you to try and make sense of what is happening to your child. Getting a diagnosis also gives some validity and is reassuring to many parents, especially if you have felt others thought you were 'making it all up' and nobody was actually listening to your concerns. Even when the diagnosis is not a positive one, parents can still feel this is better than the unknown so it's no wonder that this journey is such a desperate and stressful one.

Having support from family and friends is vital during this time. Try not to forget that they are also afraid and confused and sharing your experiences with them helps them to understand and support you. When everybody is under pressure, sharing helps to let off some steam. Give friends and family a 'job'; it makes them feel useful and needed. Many parents, mothers in particular, take on the whole burden single handed and in so doing exclude others from the journey. This often proves to be destructive to relationships and adds to the emotional angst for all. No one can do this alone and lots of people want to help and support but just do not know how to. Share your story and give others the permission to be part of it and everyone will start to feel stronger.

Our personal journey through this stage was at times terrifying and lonely. It tested our patience, resolve and relationships and I know many families have shared that experience. However looking back, I realise all the steps no matter how painful, were necessary and all part of the extraordinary course we were on. Each step we made and milestone we reached made us stronger and more resilient. It taught us to be tolerant, understanding and forgiving and best of all it made us appreciate every day and celebrate the small stuff.

Of course receiving the diagnosis initially feels like a real achievement for families. It brings huge relief, redemption and a new type of hope. At last you have a name to hang onto, something tangible. Surely now you think someone can do something? It is often a bitter sweet victory as rather than being the end of your journey you very quickly realise you have just reached first base. Time to re-group, take a deep breath and be ready to move onward and upward ☺

Chapter 3

Our gift gets a name

In our journey, five months on from the initial illness, we were about to get our diagnosis.

This was the time we were introduced to the first amazing and extraordinary person in our journey (there were many more to follow). He was to become a huge part of our lives and still is, our Respiratory Consultant from Southampton General Hospital. Here was someone at last doing something positive and proactive, carrying out tests, scans, x-rays, someone who really looked at our daughter and acknowledged that something was very wrong.

Adrenaline fuelled hope flooded our lives and at last we saw a light ahead. Being referred to our brilliant consultant enabled us to get some answers albeit hard ones. Just five months after the initial pneumonia, I first heard the words Obliterative Bronchiolitis (OB) and Bronchiectasis. It might as well have been Greek; I couldn't even pronounce it let alone spell it. Yet even hearing those words somehow was a relief, after five months of fighting to be listened to, at last someone was taking us seriously.

What is OB?
Obliterative Bronchiolitis, also known as Bronchiolitis Obliterans, is a rare and irreversible lung disease resulting from an injury to the lower respiratory tract. The small airways (bronchioles) are either completely obstructed (obliterated) or narrowed by fibrous (scar) tissue and inflammation. The condition is under recognised.

Many cases of Obliterative Bronchiolitis occur as a complication of respiratory infections such as those carried by adenovirus and mycoplasma; this is called post infectious OB. Obliterative Bronchiolitis can also occur following exposure to toxic fumes, aspiration of food/liquid, Stevens-Johnson Syndrome, collagen or vascular disease, rheumatoid arthritis and post transplant.

People with post infective OB suffer from respiratory symptoms caused by fixed narrowing of their airways. These typically include breathlessness, reduced exercise tolerance, recurrent coughing and an increased frequency of chest infections which can be difficult to treat. Co-existing lung problems are common and can be particularly troublesome. These include bronchiectasis, gastro-oesophageal reflux and difficult asthma.

I vividly remember the day our Consultant told me the diagnosis. He took me off the ward and into a side room, I knew then it was bad or he would have just sat by the bed and told me. My heart sank as the realisation of how serious it was hit home. He sat me down and scribbled out a diagram on a scrap of paper to try and explain what was happening inside my daughters' lungs. I still have that little sketch; it was the first piece of evidence that this was all real I almost felt vindicated; after all I had been telling everyone something was very wrong for many months now. My first question was. 'Well now what can we do about it?' I didn't hear much beyond the word; 'irreversible' and all I could say was 'That's not good then', as I stumbled from the room. Though I didn't realise then I was in deep shock.

I took my daughter home and began to try and make sense of this but it was just too big to comprehend. Now looking back I can see how truly alone I felt. There was nobody to talk to, nobody seemed to understand, there was no help, no information and nowhere to go. My family were all struggling with their own shock and friends had no idea what to do. I then did the worse thing I could have done. I went onto the internet and typed Obliterative Bronchiolitis into Google. All I found were worst case scenarios. I didn't understand then the difference between post – infectious OB (which my daughter has) and post transplant OB, which has a much more challenging prognosis. I spiralled into depression and despair. Now I understand that I needed to grieve and go through all the steps associated with that which I will share in a moment. Had I known that then I would have at least had some understanding of what was happening.

Many families have described to me their desperation at diagnosis time and that they felt they were out of control emotionally. At least one mother I know became so clinically depressed she needed medical help. Now I understand that this grief is 'normal'. The enormity of what is happening is just too much for your brain to comprehend and so it goes into over drive and panic, desperately trying to find solutions to a problem that it can't fix.

There is a wonderful book called 'The Chimp Paradox' by Dr Steve Peters which explains how the different parts of the human brain work and interact. The emotional part of the brain he calls the 'Chimp'.

"The Chimp is an emotional machine that thinks independently from us. It is not good or bad, it is just a Chimp" The Chimp Paradox, Dr Steve Peters, Vermillion,2011.

This Chimp is driven by emotion and survival needs and is three times stronger than the logical Human part of our brain and we have no control over it. The Chimp only has three solutions to any problem, flight, fight or freeze. It always reacts *first* to any information we receive and needs to be exercised before it will calm down and listen to the logical human part of our brain. He suggests we 'exercise the Chimp' to allow it to vent its rage as frequently and for as long as it takes and only then will it go back to sleep. For me the time after diagnosis was when the Chimp was most out of control and if I had recognised and understood that then I could have learned how to respect and manage it better.

However when I received my daughter's diagnosis I had not read this book and so my 'Chimp' was frankly hysterical most of the time despite my efforts to be rational. In the absence of any techniques or knowledge of what was happening to me it took something else to shock me back to reality.

I am by nature a 'fixer'. I like to know reasons why and find solutions and to do positive things to move forward but I just couldn't see any. Fortunately for me my daughter was strong for both of us. I had tried so hard not to get upset in front of her but one day the stress of holding it together was just too much and I broke down. My beautiful brave nine year old daughter grabbled my wrists firmly, put her little face right up to mine and in her sternest voice said ' Get a grip Mummy we have to deal with this'. It was the slap I needed and I knew I had to be the strong one for her, not the other way around for goodness sake. So I put my mind to 'dealing with it' from that moment on. Another extraordinary gift had just been delivered to me, clarity and calmness, well maybe that's two gifts?

I became more rational and purposeful. I stopped looking for that magic answer and starting taking each day at a time, celebrating each success and acknowledging each sorrow as it deserved. I knew right then and there if I couldn't make this go away for her I was going to make something positive come from this for others. Mostly I never wanted any other family to have to go through this lonely terrifying time alone as we had. The light bulb moment that was later to become Breathtakers OB Trust flickered for the first time. I knew we were going to be ok and that my daughter had truly extraordinary qualities of strength, bravery and wisdom way beyond her years and I was going to see this time and time again. She was and is my most extraordinary gift in this journey.

So let's get back to you now. Firstly reading 'The Chimp Paradox' will give you an understanding of how your brain operates, which is helpful.

> Other useful publications
>
> *Grief Counseling and Grief Therapy : a practical handbook.*
> *J William Worden*
>
> *On Grief and Grieving: Finding the meaning through the five stages of loss. Elizabeth Kubler-Ross and Daivd Kessler*

Secondly being presented with a horrible diagnosis without any support afterwards is little short of torture; however an understanding of the stages of grief will help, so let's look at them next. I wish I had known them at the time as I am sure I would have been able to cope more rationally.

The first important point is that **YES** you do need to go through all these stages. There are no short cuts but at least if you are aware of them you know what's happening to you and you can give yourself permission to feel them. It's ok; you have every right to feel these things. It can take you anything from three to twelve months or even longer to work through this. There is no right or wrong time, everyone is individual, don't beat yourself up, allow everyone to work through the process at their own pace. This is not just happening to you but to your family and friends too.

Here are the steps

- **Shock/Denial** - This is normal. Your brain can not handle this information, it is too painful and scary and unbelievable and so in self defence you go into denial. You shut down and refuse to listen to anyone. The Chimp is loose and out of control here.
- **Yearning** - A poignant and painful longing for the past, for things to just be ok again, lots of tears at this stage.

- **Bargaining** – *'If only?'* or *'If we do this?'* or *'What if we try that?'* The emotional part of your brain tries frantically to find a solution whatever the cost or no matter how unrealistic it is.
- **Anger**- Here comes that Chimp again raging with frustration, blame, injustice, unfairness and desperation to find a reason to make it less painful. You need to exercise this anger for as long as you need to. Let it out, shout, scream, and punch a pillow. You are ENTITLED to this, do it for as long and as often as you need to. You won't be able to calm the Chimp until it's worn itself out!
- **Acceptance** – Finally the emotional side of your brain begins to quieten down. The Chimp is tired now, and the logical Human part is beginning to deal with the truth and accept it. However with this calmness comes an acute sense of emptiness, a feeling of depression and hopelessness. This is real grief, you are grieving for the life you thought you were going to have with your child, all the things you thought you and they were going to do have now been changed forever. It is a deep sadness.

- **Reorganisation** - finally you accept the truths. Life is sometimes not fair. It is not fair that this has happened to your child. Goal posts do change and sometimes things are outside of your control. You are learning to live with OB and most importantly, move on in a positive way.

All these reactions are *normal* and *acceptable*; you are not going crazy or falling to pieces, although at times you think you are. It is a process that you have to work through and once you understand that and give yourself time and permission to do that, you can at least see a way forward. Don't be hard on yourself, you need time. You may have to go through the process more than once before you can move forward

> *"It may take several repeat episodes of exercising the Chimp for any one problem before you can box it"* Dr Steve Peters, The Chimp Paradox.

I truly believe that all families should be offered grief counselling after receiving a diagnosis of any serious or chronic illness, of course there is none available free for families yet. I am not a trained counselor and yet I spend much of my time supporting families at this terrible time in their lives. I listen to the heartbreaking story over and over again and it never gets any easier to hear.

My desire to help families move on and *thrive* rather than just *survive* led me to coaching. I am now a qualified life and business coach. I can offer our OB families help and guidance to move forward positively with their lives. Coaching helps families step forward, using their experiences of this journey as building blocks for the future and extracting the positive strengths they have learned along the way.

My coaching www.soaringnolimits.co.uk will proudly continue to help and support families affected by OB in the future. This is another extraordinary gift that has come my way in this strange journey and you will have them too if you open your mind to the possibilities and opportunities that you are being given.

I believe all things happen for a reason in life, even if we can never understand what that reason could possibly be. New people, opportunities and experiences will flood into your life during this time. Gifts will come along in all shapes and sizes in a relentless onslaught. Some will stay, some will only visit briefly. The first ones will seem insurmountable challenges and yet you will somehow find the strength to deal with them, you may feel at times as if you could drown in a sea of sorrow and yet gifts will come along that help you swim through. At your lowest ebb gifts of hope, love, friendship and laughter will appear just at the right moment and when you least expect them.

These wonderful gifts will be animate and inanimate but all the while they will shape and change your life and the lives of those around you. You can learn so much, grow and find peace, if you just open your eyes and heart to the possibilities.

The gifts that have filled my life throughout this process are endless. It is as if someone turned up the colour control, I don't miss a single thing. I live for today, enjoying and concentrating on the 'now' rather than the 'what if's', over which I have no control. It's time to open yourself up to the possibilities, which are infinite. OB does not have to shape or define life in a negative way, it is a set of unwanted circumstances that are challenging, but it can make you extraordinary.

Chapter 4

Diagnosis, just another milestone

When you finally get the diagnosis you have been fighting for months and sometimes years, there is an initial rush of euphoria. Now you think something is going to happen, that someone will do something and that everything will fine again. The excitement and relief is often short lived as you quickly realise what you are now facing is just more tests, more hospital appointments and more uncertainty.

For us this was also very true, we mistakenly believed that now we had the name of a disease to hang onto, this could surely all be fixed, all we had to do was find the solutions? In reality it lead to CT scans, bronchoscopy, lung function tests, it was endless. The bronchoscope examination revealed some unusual polyps in the upper airways and other tests showed gastric reflux, but despite exhaustive investigations no real virus could ever be identified for the causing the initial lung injury. Instead of giving us solutions there just seemed to be more and more questions. It also meant of course that our child was still very sick; diagnosis did not bring cure or respite, or even any real improvement in day to day health initially.

Although the acute crisis was over learning to live with chronic disease was still frightening and devastating on a daily basis.

For us it seemed that we were just adding to our list of challenges every day. Now though we had the support of our respiratory team and thanks to our great Consultant, our journey eventually took us to Great Ormond Street Hospital.

Great Ormond Street Hospital

Great Ormond Street Hospital (GOSH) is an international centre of excellence in child healthcare. Since its formation in 1852, the hospital has been dedicated to children's healthcare and to finding new and better ways to treat childhood illnesses. Each year, there are over 200,000 patient visits to the hospital. Most of the children cared for are referred from other hospitals throughout the UK and overseas. There are more than 50 different clinical specialties at GOSH. It is at the forefront of pediatric training in the UK.

Going to Great Ormond Street Hospital was another incredible and extraordinary experience for us. What an amazing place, filled with dedicated and inspiring staff. We have had several stays there including one for fundoplication surgery and I cannot praise them enough. As a parent you are made to feel that you are at the centre of everything, you are included in discussions, cared for and most importantly listened to. If you don't stay on the ward with your child, the parent hotel is convenient, spotless and enables you to be close to your child at all times.

> **Nissen Fundoplication** - *a surgical procedure in which the upper portion of the stomach is wrapped around the lower end of the esophagus and sutured in place as a treatment for the reflux of stomach contents into the oesophagus.*

What we found at Great Ormond Street was peace of mind and reassurance; it felt like it was no longer a fight, almost as if everyone was finally on the same playing field, heading for the same goal. The care we received was world class and for a place full of sick children everywhere you looked there were smiling faces and friendly people. The hospital brims with hope and joy which is infectious.

What we didn't find was that 'magic cure'. That I admit was somewhat of a shock. We went to Great Ormond Street believing they could fix anything, and talking to other families many others feel the same.

Looking back it was all part of the long road to acceptance which was necessary but sometimes difficult to travel. It did bring a sense of great reassurance though that we had explored every avenue and that we had not missed anything that may have been possible. We now knew that we were doing the best we could and it helped us create a clearer framework for the future.

For many parents it's the 'not knowing' that is the hardest thing to come to terms with. I know some who have wasted years pursuing 'the elusive answer', desperately trying to establish time lines and probabilities and consequently their lives have been miserable. This is so sad and my heart goes out to them, my advice for your sake and your child's is to STOP trying to predict the future. In truth none of us know what tomorrow will bring, we don't expect to know if we may be run over by a bus next week or win the lottery and it is an unrealistic expectation to imagine anyone can give you a completely reliable prediction of your child's future with OB. We have no idea what medical innovations may emerge over the next few years or decades and in honesty there has simply not been enough research done around this disease yet to know all the future possibilities. I find focusing on each day and enjoying each moment to be much more beneficial. If I want to direct my energy to finding answers, I do it by raising awareness of this disease with medical professionals and encouraging research. The more people who know about this disease, the more likely new pathways of treatment will emerge. As parents our voice is our power so let's use it in the most proactive way possible. Tell your story everywhere and to anyone who will listen, you just never know where those ripples will go.

You are simply not going to find that definitive answer so instead try to live every day and celebrate every occasion. Don't let this disease steal away the joy of simply enjoying your child every single day.

I think for many parents the realisation that simply having a name of a disease doesn't necessarily solve the problems is difficult to rationalise and can trigger a whole new spiral of confusion and despair. It's like one step forward and one step back, again don't worry that's normal. Go back to the steps of grief we talked about in the previous chapter, let that Chimp out for a bit more exercise and then you can move on confidently and with hope.

Chapter 5

Breathtakers OB Trust

It had taken me a long time of struggling alone before I realized that something simply had to done to help OB families. In 2007 I had still only met one other family affected by OB, I understood little about the disease and could not find anybody who could help me. For us at that time it just seemed like more and more bad news. There were numerous hospital admissions, referral to Great Ormond Street Hospital which resulted in fundoplication surgery for gastric reflux, an added diagnosis of bronchiectasis and so much medicine I could have opened my own chemist shop.

There was also the nightmare struggle with school (more on that later), some horrific hospital scenarios, financial stress from only one income in the house and the juggling act of trying to hold family and friend relationships together. All in all a crazy time and amongst all this chaos my daughter was trying to deal with these massive changes to her life with no professional emotional support.

The idea of doing 'something' had been niggling away in the back of my mind for over a year now and the final definitive 'Breathtakers' moment came as I sat one day having a cup of coffee looking out of my conservatory window, on my own yet again, while the rest of the world seemed to be getting on with living. I was so fed up of feeling helpless and alone, I decided I had to start a support group for families. I had been told there were other families out there I just needed to find them. I had no idea how do to it or even where to start but I could clearly see what I wanted to achieve and so believed from that moment without a doubt it could be done. I had a dream to create a network of families supporting each other and raising awareness of OB. I desperately didn't want any other family to go through the misery that we had experienced, on their own.

I ran the idea past my family who seemed to think it was a good idea. Although perhaps in hindsight they just thought it would be good for me to 'do' something. My daughter and I discussed it at length and she was my biggest supporter as ever and we brainstormed some ideas. Suddenly we felt very pioneering and excited and this was great positive energy for us both.

So I went back to Google. Last time my searches only brought bad news but this time they brought ideas and possibilities. I discovered that to start a charity I needed to raise £3000 and find two other people to be Trustees. I soon met another one of the many extraordinary people that this OB journey was going to bring into my life.

One of the teaching assistants at my daughter's primary school was a lovely vivacious lady called Karen, who had always been kind and positive. I did not know her very well then but she was always very supportive of my daughter. I approached her nervously to ask if she would consider being a trustee of the charity. She never even blinked at what must have seemed a crazy idea from someone who knew not the first thing about starting a charity and who was frankly a bit of an emotional mess at the time. Her unfailing and unwavering support has been constant over the past eight years. She is probably not even aware of how much she helped me, especially in those early and uncertain days of the charity; however her ability to 'creatively play the devil's advocate' and remain bubbly and positive no matter what life threw at us, was and still is priceless.

I didn't know it then but this unwanted adventure would bring many more amazing and dynamic people into my life, just some of the gifts this disease would give.

To register the charity I discovered somehow I had to raise £3000. I had never done any serious fundraising but my daughter was the first to come forward with an idea and she held a fantastic crazy hair day event which appeared in the local newspaper and on the radio and helped raise the funds. Kiri's Dad and two brothers, family, friends and another lady who had a son with OB ran the London 10K marathon and we reached the magic £3000. By 2008 Breathtakers was a registered charity, it had begun.

This was also my first real lesson that if you just decide to do something that you totally believe in, it will happen somehow, no matter what the obstacles are. I have used this principle many times over since with the charity, I just decide the project, don't worry about the 'how' and the funds and means to carry it out appear and it does happen. I guess it's all about not sweating the small stuff.

Just to digress many people ask me where the name Breathtakers comes from. One of the first people I came into contact with who had OB was a young lady then aged 17. She became a complete inspiration for me. She had been poorly since she was 13 and I spoke with her at length over the next few years via email about her journey, her fears, her hopes and the charity. She used the word 'Breathtaking' in her emails, it seemed so appropriate that I asked if I could use the idea for the charity name. Sadly she has since passed away but her courage and dignity was inspirational, she touched so many lives and worked passionately to the end to encourage organ donation. She will never be forgotten by those who knew her and many who didn't. She shared her story, often painful and heartbreaking to raise understanding and awareness of this disease and she never let her illness compromise her beliefs. The name Breathtakers will always be a poignant reminder for me of her and the encouragement she gave me at a time when she was going through so much herself.

So what now? We had a name and a charity registration number so next I needed to make contact with other families and doctors and I knew a website was a must. First I had to get funds for a laptop and had my first tentative attempt at applying for grants from trust funds. Amazingly I got the £600 I needed, another example of belief bringing the means, and so the next step was a website. With no funds to pay a web developer realized I had to do this myself but had no idea how. It's amazing what you can teach yourself to do when you are driven and within a few short weeks of working into the midnight hours our website went live. It wasn't fantastic but it did the trick and became our shop window to the world, the first OB portal.

It was a tense and nerve wracking time. What if nobody looked at it? What if nobody got in touch? What if all the hard work had been for nothing? Deep down I knew it would work, after all here was the very website that I had been searching for myself for the past two years but could never find, I knew there would be others doing just the same thing.

I was right.

In the first month the site had over 400 hits, I received emails from 11 families all desperate for contact with other OB families, all of them experiencing the same fears and loneliness I was. From feeling completely lost and powerless suddenly I was empowered, knowing I was doing something so positive that would help other families.

In that first year alone Breathtakers reached out to more than 20 families. For me that was amazing because I had believed we were one of the *only* families in the UK. The network of support began to thrive and more people began to discover their own hope, that wonderful vessel that was going to carry them through it all. I began to make amazing relationships with other families many of which are still strong today. We held each other's hands, were there for each other when we needed to cry and laughed together at the joys. We began to feel the power of sharing this journey and for me it was a huge driving force to continue what I'd started.

This was also an important time for our OB children, because suddenly they could see that there were others just like them, children who were experiencing all the same challenges and fears and they knew now that they were not alone. Families began to post their story on the website and photographs appeared of these amazing children. The OB family had begun to grow. As adults we are often so engrossed with our own struggle with this journey we forget the impact on our children, they too are trying to make sense of their strange and scary world. As children they look to their parents to make everything right and yet often those very people are lost and confused too, it must be terrifying for them. Now they could begin to contact and talk to other children and share their experiences and gain strength from each other.

Initially my idea had been to provide support for families, to give them reliable information, to facilitate contact between them and create a thriving and safe place for families to share their stories, fears and questions. Once that all began to happen beautifully I began to see what else Breathtakers could achieve.

Raising awareness with doctors became my next objective, as I realized that our early experiences, when nobody had even heard of OB let alone knew what to do with it, were not confined to us. Nearly every family I spoke to told me the same story regarding lack of knowledge and awareness of this disease.

Before diagnosis some families had had to battle for many months (in one case years) with their GP to get a referral to a specialist. I personally had many GP confrontations where I simply felt I was seen as a neurotic mother. For some families inaction by GP's had led to emergency admissions to PICU, in three cases I know, of requiring ventilation. Our own journey started when, in my opinion, a GP did not do his job adequately.

Families were telling me about the stress of misdiagnosis and it was very clear that support after diagnosis with OB was also variable. However how could doctors treat OB effectively if they had no idea what it was or how to recognize it? Many parents described scenarios where they were the ones explaining the disease to bemused medical staff and how terrifying that felt.

Later in our 2010 survey we discovered that only 41% of families believed that their GP provided adequate support. Of the others, 59% said they either *'never'* or *'hardly ever'* see their GP as they felt it was a waste of time and the majority felt their GP had little or no knowledge of OB. This had and has been my own experience with GP's too and I rarely, if ever, bother visiting them.

Fighting to get flu jabs, seemed a common occurrence, difficulties over repeat prescriptions was viewed as the norm. Overall the families expressed serious concerns about the levels of care, knowledge and poor practice offered by their GP's. Most distressing were incidences of GP's *'not believing'* parents regarding their child's condition and refusal to refer onto specialists despite persistent requests from parents, which sometimes had devastating results for individual families

One family had waited ten years before OB had been diagnosed and for those ten years they had been desperately telling doctors that something was very wrong, that their child was never well and that all those inhalers and steroids were doing nothing. They had for ten years repeated their story over and over again, been driven to despair and made to feel they were lying or exaggerating about their child's illness.

Later our 2010 survey revealed that persistence by families was a key factor and some families felt they had had to 'fight' to get a diagnosis. 43% of the families surveyed received a misdiagnosis, the most common being asthma. The whole process of dealing with medical professionals at every level was very traumatic and stressful for some families and it mostly seemed to come down to lack of knowledge.

> 'We had to fight to see a consultant; it was exhausting just to get there. The GP was insistent it was asthma'. Mum of OB Child.

> 'I was sent home and told to ignore the wheezing....I feel that medication could have been given quicker and CT scan should have been done sooner and the damage to his lungs could have been prevented' Mum of OB child.

However those survey results came much later in 2010, back in 2008 I was not aware of the scale of the problem. All I knew was that was more and more families were relaying their own particular horror stories to me and that there was an obvious and very clear need to raise awareness with medical professionals on all levels. A picture also began to emerge that care, recognition and treatment in some areas of the UK was far superior than in other areas. I realised that raising awareness was vital if I wanted families to get equal and high quality support across the UK.

Initially I personally contacted every respiratory centre and respiratory consultant I could find in the UK, I sent leaflets and information and began to establish great relationships with key medical professionals. The response was mixed at first; interestingly the consultants who were already recognising and caring for OB patients really well were the most receptive and supportive. However those who had either not come into contact with the disease or had families I knew of who were not happy with the treatment they were receiving were less enthusiastic and more suspicious of us. This was a challenge as they were the very professionals I wanted to engage with. Persistence as ever was the key, so I began a long campaign of information dispersal, which still continues. I try to have a presence at conferences, in journals, in organizations, basically anywhere where our profile may be seen. I love it now when families contact me and say they have been referred from their consultant as it confirms that we are doing it right and getting somewhere at last. I was told by one consultant that for him to be able to direct a family to us for support is a great help, especially straight after diagnosis, when families are most confused and upset.

So now the Breathtakers family was growing and as a charity we were beginning to be known amongst medical professionals. We developed family information packs, awareness leaflets and redesigned our website to make it more effective. Facebook and Twitter began to play a role and our reach began to stretch overseas. Suddenly I had families from America, Australia, New Zealand and India contacting me and I realized yet again how unknown this disease was and how little support was available worldwide. Our OB family was becoming international now and yet from wherever in the world families contacted me they all seemed to be facing the same challenges, lack of information, misdiagnosis and no network of support.

I discovered that there was a large population of children in South America with OB and established a relationship with doctors there. I had never dreamt when this idea began that I would be talking with doctors from as far afield as Australia, Canada and

USA. There was and is still so much to learn and to do.

Of course like every charity we had to have funds to carry out this work and so our fundraising efforts have had to keep growing and finding new avenues to support us. I think we've done it all now from charity Balls to race days, sponsored runs to cream teas, recycling to auctions. Our orange and black shirts are becoming a very familiar sight in my home town. Mostly it's fun but it's also exhausting and time consuming; which is why we are so very grateful to our wonderful OB families who support us with their own fundraising efforts. I cannot stress enough that we would not be here without you, you know who you are, too many to list but a HUGE thank you and please, please, please, keep supporting us. Every penny you raise goes to helping children with OB, our children.

Funds aside, fund raising has been another enlightening and empowering gift for me. I had never really been involved in any serious way before in trying to establish funding sustainability in this way. The process has pushed me way outside my own comfort zone many times over the years, increased my confidence, and given me a new perspective on people. Having to approach strangers and 'sell your story' in a persuasive way is challenging, all those 'no's' are hard to take at first and it's tough not to get disillusioned but overall you develop new communication skills and an inner resilience. Every 'no' is now just a step nearer to that 'yes' for me, so now I actually thank people for saying 'no, it throws them totally!

What fundraising has also done has allowed me to witness the true and selfless generosity of people. Anyone who tells you that people don't care in this world must have their eyes closed. I have been and continue to be astounded by people and their endless capacity for giving both in terms of time and finance. The list of incredible people who consistently give their time and expertise to Breathtakers is long but Joanne our North East parent contact who has been with us almost from day one, our enthusiastic Trustees Sue, Karen and Steve, Sam our innovative and brilliant 'techy' guy (and so much more), your support is priceless. Rachel and Kerrie, who are my left and right hand respectively and keep me smiling and laughing constantly and keep the Breathtakers wheels turning daily.

I have had people who don't even know me press £1000 into my hand unexpectedly, children who hand over their 50p pocket money and pensioners who give me £1 that they probably can't afford to give simply because they have been moved by our story. People have big hearts and I am blessed to have witnessed such joyous giving.

I have learnt that by simply telling your story you can send out ripples far and wide, that you never know who is listening and that the results of that can be unexpected and enormous, that by never talking about the 'cash' but concentrating on the 'cause', the support you receive is phenomenal and that in general people not only care but if they can help, they will. Words are powerful, words said with genuine passion are profound and life changing. Just tell your story to anyone who will listen.

Through this part of the journey I have met so many different, interesting and inspiring people from all walks of life who ordinarily I would never had had the opportunity or privilege to get to know from mountain climbers to merchant bankers, motivational speakers to medical pioneers, courageous children and charismatic characters, the famous faces and fantastic families, those who survived and those who thrive despite all that is thrown at them, all of whom have shaped and changed me with their experiences. What a gift and I am so grateful for it.

Our mission at the Trust is *'Simply to make life better for people with OB'* and I remain as firmly committed to that now as I did back in 2007. However the amazing people and circumstances I have been fortunate enough to be exposed to since then, have not only strengthened my resolve and determination to make a lasting and profound difference to the way OB is recognised and treated but in turn these amazing people have *'Simply made my life better'* too.

Chapter 6

Breathtakers Route Map

In 2010 Breathtakers were chosen to be one of only ten UK charities to be part of a unique project with the Genetic Alliance, funded by the Department of Health to create a route map of rare disease. I grabbed this opportunity with zeal; another amazing gift had just come my way.

Being chosen to be part of the route map project was very exciting for Breathtakers and gave us an opportunity to explore and develop new ways of disseminating information to families and medical professionals. However it also presented challenges for a small organization in terms of how we would manage from a 'man-power' perspective. After much thought it was decided that it would be main project for me 2010 and that we would somehow work out how everything else would be done as we went along. Not very scientific but working under pressure seems to work well for us as an organization.

So myself and Sue (our then brilliant volunteer, now Trustee) started to brainstorm exactly how to undertake this huge task. I think we were both initially unprepared for the sheer size and scope of the project, what started out with seemingly clear parameters soon spread out like a spider's web in all directions. We spent many hours to begin with simply drawing mind maps on A1 paper. It became apparent that we had to have very clear areas and limits or we would never be able to achieve a cohesive map.

To ensure that we were on the right track on the content for the map we conducted a national survey of OB families, the first one of its kind.

The survey looked at areas of both concern and excellence and gave us an idea of what families needed to know. We also had meetings with the respiratory medical team from Southampton Hospital to brainstorm ideas for medical content. Though this was invaluable in terms of accuracy of information it also presented challenges in getting agreement on wordings (too many differing opinions) and timescale issues (medical team very busy). However overall in terms of validity of information and accuracy the medical team input was vital.

We decided early on the design of how we wanted the Route Map to look (flow chart) and this decision also helped us clearly define each section and break it down into more manageable projects chunks. Working with our web designer Sam we began to design the way we wanted the map to look and function.

We then started the long and hard research process, taking each section in turn finding the key information and relevant links and supporting information. I wrote the text for each section and Sue painstakingly proof read and checked all web links and research papers (many times over). As each section was finished it was emailed to Sam who started to populate the map. This was a true team effort and very exciting as it started to take shape before our eyes.

Once the map was fully populated the proof reading process began again to ensure it was all working and correct, another very time consuming process as we addressed functionality issues. We then sent the map out to various families and doctors for them to 'test drive' and again addressed any issues or comments. This proved interesting and important especially as it threw up one area we had completely overlooked and so once this had been identified we then added to the map. So we discovered more eyes, were definitely better than four eyes, in this case.

There were definite lows along the way, mostly due to a lack of time. It was a lot of work and added to other pressures of running the charity and it was quite stressful sometimes. There were the frustrations of researching and gaining 'rights' to use the information in map. In reality there was not enough funding for the project it only happened because most work was absorbed 'in house' and voluntarily.

The overall highs though overshadowed any concerns and constraints we encountered. Seeing it all come together and realizing what an amazing tool it would be was incredible. Building great working relationships with Sue and Sam along the way was another big plus for me; yes it was fun sometimes too.

So our map was launched and was a great milestone for Breathtakers and OB. It has now gone all over the world, been used at medical conferences in Australia and USA and for training purposes and presentations in the UK with medical students. Better still families are using it and finding clear and accurate information when they need it most. It's a one-stop-shop that they can dip in and out of on their OB journey.

Its purpose is to be empowering, informing and caring, a complete clinical and social care pathway for the journey of Obliterative Bronchiolitis. A living resource for patients, families and professionals when planning care based on best practice; to improve access to information, encourage early diagnosis, foster effective development of new services, promote national standards and raise awareness of OB. For me it ticks all those boxes and more and has been a great achievement for the charity. Back in 2007 two of the initial objectives of the charity were to provide accurate and reliable information to families and to raise awareness with medical professionals, here we have found a way to do both of those things and much more effectively and innovatively.

We are continuing to explore ways of disseminating the map in beneficial ways and because it is a 'living resource' we review and update it constantly. You can view the whole route map at:
http://www.routemap.breathtakers.org.uk/

The map has been just another innovative way we have found at the OB Trust to accomplish our mission of 'Simply making life better for people with OB'.

Another great and extraordinary gift.

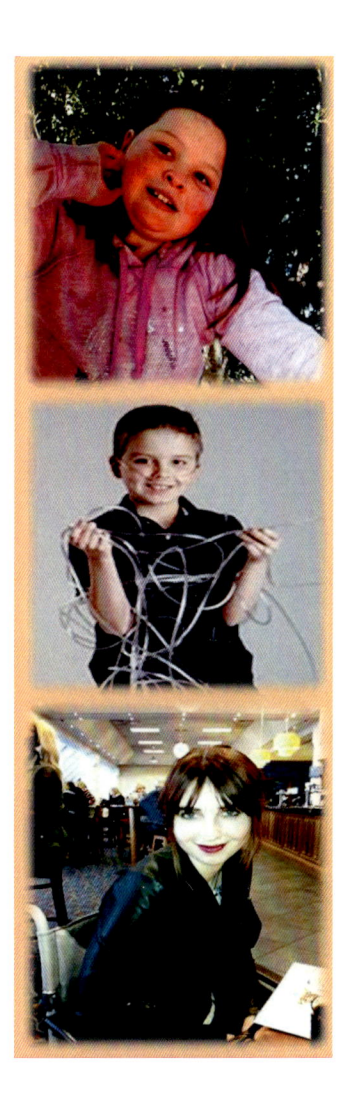

Our Superstars

Our Superstars

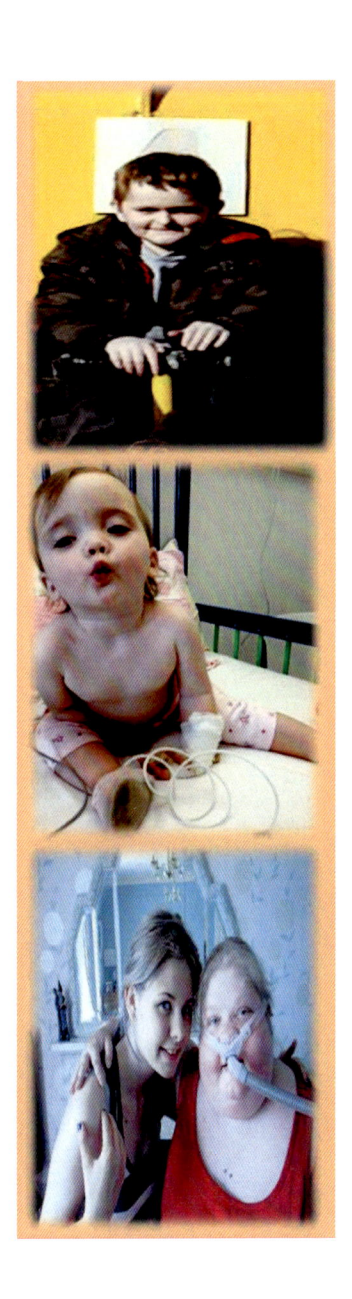

Our Superstars

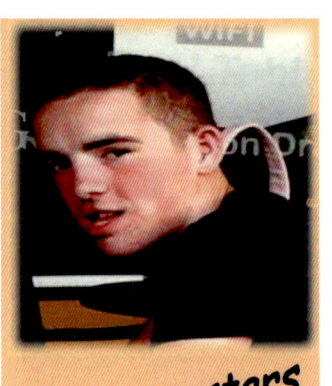

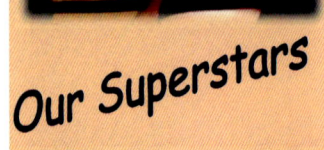

Our Superstars

Our Superstars

Obliterative Bronchiolitis (OB) Route Map

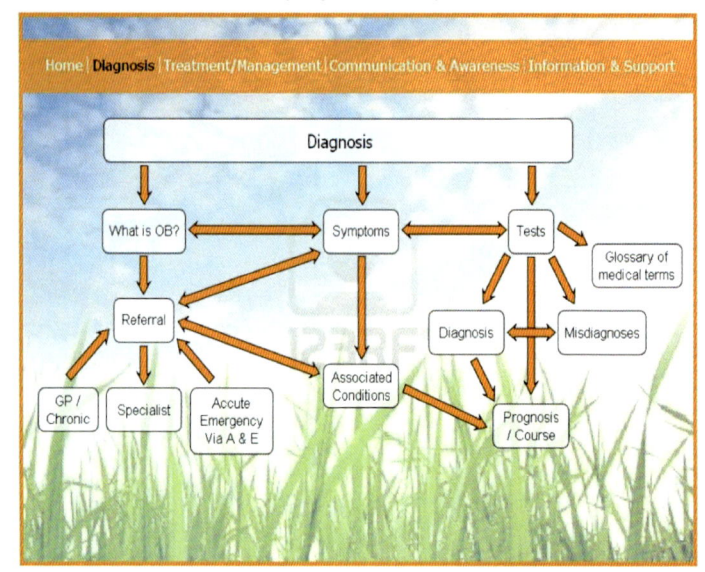

www.routemap.breathtakers.org.uk

'Empowering-Informing-Caring'

A clinical and social care pathway for the complete journey of Obliterative Bronchiolitis (OB)

Also known as Bronchiolitis Obliterans

Chapter 7

Hospital Experiences

> 'Lack of interest by many nurses as to what is actually wrong with their patients is scary...even when it's obvious they know nothing, they still don't listen and just do their own thing'. Mum of OB child.

On our journey I started to learn about the sometimes unpleasant side of hospital experiences. There are many wonderful doctors and nurses, and the majority of the care we have received has been fantastic but this story would not be true or complete without the less than positive experiences as well as the positive and so I make no apology for the truth as it helps us learn and move forward.

We often hear talk in the media about the falling standards in nursing care, the lack of compassion and professionalism. It's easy to get caught up in all that and I understand that for those good nurses who are out there, which I am sure are in the majority, it must be infuriating and disheartening. However when you have a sick child you don't care about the good nurses, after all that's what you expect, that's what they should all be like, you only remember the bad ones.

Sadly poor hospital experiences are not unique nor are the problems confined to a particular hospital. When Breathtakers OB Trust carried out a family survey in 2010, it revealed many worrying concerns over hospital ward care. We discovered other families all over the UK had their own horror stories to relate.

A survey of 2254 nurses in 2012 showed that the UK nurses themselves are worried over the falling standards of their own profession. When rating standards generally, the majority (58 %) described the standard as either 'mediocre', 'low' or 'worryingly low'.

Following the publication of the Francis report of the Mid Staffordshire NHS Trust Foundation Public Inquiry on 6th February 2013 the government published its own response on 3rd April 2013. Their report 'Putting Patients First' states that the quality of patient care will be put at the heart of the NHS in an overhaul of health and care.

You can find more information about this at: https://www.gov.uk/government/news/putting-patients-first-government-publishes-response-to-francis-report

Jeremy Hunt said:

The events at Stafford Hospital were a betrayal of the worst kind. A betrayal of the patients, of the families, and of the vast majority of NHS staff who do everything in their power to give their patients the high quality, compassionate care they deserve.

The health and care system must change. We cannot merely tinker around the edges – we need a radical overhaul with high quality care and compassion at its heart. Today I am setting out an initial response to Robert Francis' recommendations. But this is just the start of a fundamental change to the system.

I can pledge that every patient will be treated in a hospital judged on the quality of its care and the experience of its patients. They will be cared for in a place with a culture of zero harm, by highly trained staff with the right values and skills. And if something should go wrong, then those mistakes will be admitted, the patient told about them and steps taken to rectify them with proper accountability.

I and the chairs of key organisations involved in care have pledged to do this and make our health and care system the best and safest in the world.

More recently the government has found itself in a bitter dispute with the Royal College of Nursing over plans to shake up nursing training by having nurses work for a year as nursing assistants, feeding, washing and dressing patients. Whatever your views are on this issue I think everyone would agree that all patients should be treated with care, dignity and respect and all patients should be safe whilst in hospital care.

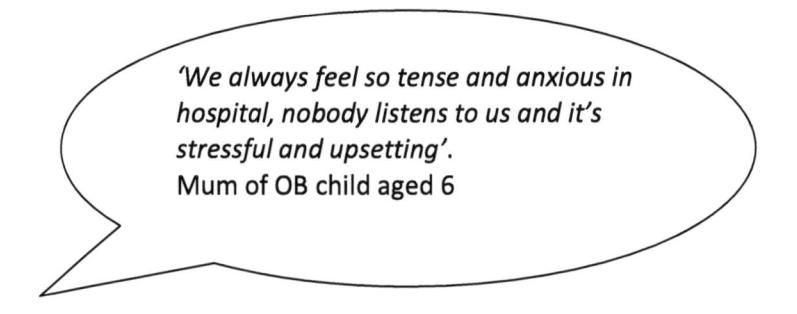

> 'We always feel so tense and anxious in hospital, nobody listens to us and it's stressful and upsetting'.
> Mum of OB child aged 6

So what can we do to try and make things easier and less stressful during hospital encounters which after all are part of life on this journey? OB families know that hospital admissions are a fact, they are sometimes just going to happen, but if we go into them in the right frame of mind they can be so much less frustrating and depressing with a happier outcome.

So here's a few ways to take angst out it all and just chill a bit.

Be Prepared

Go to every appointment prepared to stay in overnight, you can always just take the bag home and unpack again, accept that unscheduled overnight stays happen. It only takes five minutes to pack an overnight bag and chuck it in the car boot when you head off for an appointment or even and A and E visit. There is nothing more stressful that being sent up to the ward and thinking you've not got any clean clothes, money, tooth brush etc. You only need enough for one night after that someone can sort you out from home. If you do stay you can feel smug for being so organized and if you don't have to stay you feel great taking that bag home and unpacking, it's a victory either way.

Always have with you a written statement or letter of your child's or your diagnosis, a list of medications and the name of your regular consultant and contact number. This saves SO much stress especially if you are in different hospital than normal or you have had an A and E admission. Many medical staff, in an Accident and Emergency department, will probably not know what OB is and will be grateful of the information. Accident and Emergency is where so many parents and patients really lose control, frustrations boil over and everyone gets so upset. After all you are scared and what you want is fast effective treatment and often that's the last thing you get because nobody understands what is really wrong. Having this information also avoids all those pointless tests to rule out 'other things' that you know are a total waste of time, but the staff, have to do in the absence of correct diagnosis. This is all doubly important if you go on holiday abroad, always be prepared for the worst and if anything does happen you will at least be ready for it and its one less thing to worry about.

Polite but firm, the only way!

Telling your story over and over again to new medical staff is soul destroying, so again this is where you're facts list is great, just give them a copy. I now refuse to keep on and on filling in ward admission forms. I politely ask them to refer to the notes of which there is a stack as big as a sky scraper of previous admission forms detailing everything they need to know. Obviously if things have changed you need to inform them but yet another nurse asking you '*so when did you first get a cough?*' is not necessary and produces instant and avoidable fury.

Never feel intimated by staff, you are the best expert on your child or your own disease. Firm politeness is always the best route but if it fails don't be afraid to simply say no. Ask to see another doctor or your consultant and don't be bullied. Poor nursing, sadly is a reality sometimes, but don't let it affect you because you are too polite or don't feel you can do anything about it. People can only make you feel bad if you give them permission to do so. You might not be able to change their behavior but you CAN change your response to it.

So if things like medications and IV's are supposed to be given four hourly and you find five or six hours pass and they haven't been done, don't just sit and fume go and ask and then insist if necessary. If your child has been missed out on the lunch trolley, don't just say nothing and buy something from the shop. If you know your child is in pain don't just be fobbed off with '*oh I'll be there in a minute*' or '*oh it'll be fine*'. It is far more stressful to *not* act than to take control and do something. That doesn't mean you have to be abusive or shout but if you are assertive and persistent you will soon find that the ward staff respond to that and you don't get ignored. Take deep breath and relax.

I made a promise to myself very early on the OB journey that I would never behave in a way that caused any detriment or pain or stress to my daughter just because it was easier than causing a fuss. That I owed it her to be her champion and that by giving anything less I was letting her and myself down. Now she is more than capable of being assertive herself as she has followed my lead and I never have to worry about how she may be treated if I am not there. I am always polite and hopefully there isn't a big red note on the files saying *'Beware the Mother'* though they do all know me in Respiratory Department which is no bad thing.

You can only get stressed and upset by others if you allow them to treat you in a disrespectful way so don't give them permission to do that in first place.

Jargon Buster

Dealing with hospital jargon is also fairly stressful, doctors can sometimes seem as if they are speaking another language and this can make us escalate the seriousness of something because we just don't understand it. Ask the doctor to explain to you in plain English because if you don't say that you can't understand they will just assume you do. Don't rely on the nurse to translate either once the doctor has gone, chances are they might not know either.

Often we sit around in anticipation waiting for hours for 'The Doctors Rounds' and then they seem to be in and out in a flash and we are no wiser as to what is happening. Try and write a list of questions that you want to ask before they come around and ask them to explain properly what's happening. If you don't ask they probably will not elaborate or will just assume that you know what you need to. If you are really confused ask if they can set aside a time to talk to you later maybe in their office on a one-to-one basis. Often people revere doctors and feel they don't have a right to ask questions, this is absolute nonsense; doctors are just people who happen to know about medicine. If there was something wrong with your dog you would have no qualms about questioning the vet in great detail about what could it be, or your child's teacher if you felt they were behind at school. Your doctor is no different but if you don't ask they can't read your mind. You need to take the responsibility of finding out what you need know. If you can't get an answer that satisfies you ask for second opinion until you are satisfied you have all the facts.

Rise above the moaners

Don't get dragged into what I call hospital bashing with other mothers, fathers or patients, it's just a downhill spiral. We've all sat there in the waiting rooms or on the wards for long hours and listened to others continually moaning and whining about how long they've been waiting to see the doctor or what that nurse did wrong. It's so depressing and achieves nothing except to bring everyone's mood down, especially the patient. If you go into hospital always expecting a poor experience you can bet you'll always get one. If you have got an issue, deal with it but don't make everybody else's day a misery too.

Go prepared for long waits. You know it's going to happen so take some games, cards and books with you. Time passes so much quicker if you are doing something positive instead of clock watching and then getting angry about clock watching. Instead of having negative conversations with others around you, talk about something pleasant, I've met some really lovely and interesting people at hospitals. Try and get out of the habit of feeling that if you're at hospital it's somehow compulsory to be miserable.

Get friends and family to come and give you break, even enough time just to go for a walk off the ward or go for a coffee. One of the nicest things anyone did for us when my daughter had been in hospital for a couple of weeks was bring us some delicious Marks and Spencer food all packed beautifully with plates and knives and forks and send us off the ward for a couple of hours to just eat something really nice and relax. We came back revived and smiling and able to carry on.

Bring home in with you

De-hospitalize your stay. Take you own pillow into hospital (so much nicer) and ear plugs if you can't sleep through the beeping machines and four hourly observations. Anything you find comforting may help such as hot chocolate, your slippers, your own drinks mug and your favorite perfume. Make your little bed area or room 'your space'. My daughter often used to take photographs when she was younger of her brothers or friends, especially if it is was for a prolonged stay. All these small things are empowering and make you feel safer and more in charge.

Take care of yourself, have a shower, put some make up on and dress in something comfortable but smart and nice. Don't slop around in that old tatty track suit which will just make you feel even worse. Instead lift your whole mood by feeling better about yourself. Do the same for your child, make them feel nice, brush their hair, massage their back, just sit and cuddle. Tactile activities are so beneficial for both of you .I discovered at one stage that reflexology helped my daughter relax and feel better. After taking her for a few sessions I decided I could learn to do it myself and went off to our local college and qualified to become a reflexologist. That was then something I could use both in hospital and at home to help relax her and just make things better. It is a lovely way for us to connect and makes her feel special. Use whatever you can to feel comfortable and safe.

I remember once being in a four bed ward with a lady whose teenage son had been in a rugby accident at school, he had broken his neck and was in a very bad way. He was not going to walk again and his dream had been to be an international sports man. Every single day she breezed into the ward looking fabulous, hair done, make up immaculate and smiling brightly and everyday everyone in that ward smiled too as she came in. She lifted everyone's mood, especially her son. She refused to believe his life was over and was already looking at a rehabilitation centre he could go to enable him to train and make the best of his potential. The whole time she talked to him about things they were going to do and places they were going. No matter how bad things are there is always something good to look forward to, sometimes it's just not what we originally planned. I truly believe that positivity always impacts and improves outcomes and is something we should all practice every day even, or maybe especially, in hospital.

Smile while you plan your escape

If you have to be in hospital, at least try to keep smiling, while you are there. People watch, it is great fun and helps to while away the hours. Keep a journal, write a book about your experiences and use the time constructively. You have no choice about being there but you do have a choice as to how you feel when you are there. If you are happy, you're child will be too.

Many hospitals have clowns or magicians that visit the children's wards and once when we were there a man and his dog came in, everybody was smiling for hours afterwards. If your child is able to escape the ward for walk outside or visit home, take it. Just a change of scenery for an hour or so helps so much. My daughter rather enjoyed the celebrity status of being in MacDonald's drip, tubes, cannula's and all !!

Finally just SMILE, learn to laugh at the little annoying things and plan your escape of course and all the great things you are going to do once you are discharged.

Chapter 8

School learning curves

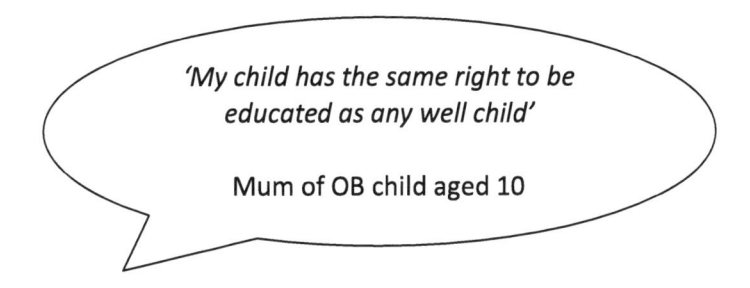

> *'My child has the same right to be educated as any well child'*
>
> Mum of OB child aged 10

When your child is sick and off school with a cold or chicken pox or something similar you expect that fairly shortly they will be recovering and everything be back to normal. A week or two of missed work is soon overcome and thankfully our children are not usually sick too often in a year.

When your child is normally healthy you never really consider the consequences of having a child who because of chronic disease regularly misses an awful lot of school. Initially you may have no strategy for dealing with the missed work, the loneliness, the depression and long term social effects and you quickly discover that your school possibly does not have a strategy either.

Added to the medical worries, financial strains and relationship challenges you suddenly find yourself with another dimension of concern and yet again out of your comfort zone.

Some schools are great and very supportive others are not. If you get a supportive school it's fabulous, if you get a bad one it's a nightmare but don't despair there are solutions to every challenge.

My daughter's primary school proved to be dire. Although some of the staff were sympathetic the head teacher was not, in fact he was so bad I eventually had to call in the LEA (Local Education Authority) to try and arbitrate. Once it became apparent that my daughter's illness was not just going to go away and that the school were going to have to go the extra mile to support her, it just became a constant battle. The school failed to accommodate her needs and in fact when it was sport or outside activities she was usually left in a classroom on her own or sent to do photocopying. She felt she was being punished for being ill. After many long hard battles I finally managed to secure extra tutoring for four hours a week and the rest of the time I home schooled her but I soon discovered that when she went into school for her one-to-one time she was in fact either doing chores like stapling papers or tidying books and was rarely actually doing any work or catch up. The whole experience was depressing for her and resulted in her being socially excluded from her peers and was nerve wracking and emotionally charged for me.

Most sharp learning curves result in great new skills being acquired fast. This was no exception for me and as usual I refused to come out of the situation without a positive. All the things I learned I made sure I passed on to other families to make sure they didn't have to go through the same miserable scenario. On the Breathtakers website and Route map there are whole sections on school and how to deal with it in the best and most productive way for everyone involved. Breathtakers also provide educational leaflets for parents to take into school to help explain OB and how the school can best support your child.

Our survey in 2010 revealed that school was a challenge for a lot of OB families. The main findings showed that in relation to school support 32% felt that overall understanding and adaptability at their child's school was totally inadequate. For 24% attendance issues were difficult, upsetting and an ongoing problem. These were the same families who felt overall they did not get adequate support from their schools in other areas.

Often schools seem to cope well on a day to day basis but there is lack of long term planning and strategy. 76% of the families with school age children reported that the school had no plan or strategy regarding catching up after absences, arranging for work to be sent home or methods for keeping the child engaged with school socially and educationally during prolonged absences. This was despite the fact that 46% of families had had meetings to establish such a plan which was then in reality **not** carried through. 54% had never had a meeting at school to discuss a plan or strategy for their child's OB.

Schools were often unaware or did not put into place provisions that could be made to support older pupils such as reduced curriculum, extra exam time and separate exam rooms.

For children who were oxygen dependant school experiences were generally reported as very good. 76% reported that their school or nursery was supportive and had a written policy in place for dealing with an oxygen dependent child in the school.

This finding was not surprising as for children who are oxygen dependant there is a very visual daily reminder of the challenges.

Other children with OB who are not oxygen dependant are often described generally by people as *'looking really well'* or *'you'd never know anything was wrong'*. If I had a pound for every time I heard that one I'd be a millionaire! Though as a parent this is frustrating and sometimes upsetting, people do generally make judgments by what they see and if there is no physical evidence people often find it difficult to empathise. Whilst this may be understandable for strangers there is no excuse for this with school staff who are well informed about your child's condition. In fact I believe it should make them more aware and observational of your child's needs. Constant reminders and persistent contact with an unsupportive school is the only way to make progress no matter how emotionally draining this is. It is important to champion your child to ensure they get the best because if you don't no else will. You don't have to win any popularity prizes with the staff and remember they are paid to give your child an education just like every other child.

Our survey confirmed that overall 'positive experiences' at school were often driven by the parent, the more input and consistent contact the parent had, the better the outcome and I certainly found this to be the case. If it's not good enough, shout about it, until someone listens.

By the time my daughter was ready for secondary school we were well equipped with the tools we needed to interact successfully with the school. It was easier for the school and us as we went in with a very clear idea of what we wanted and how it could all work out for the best. My daughter had five happy years in a supportive and encouraging environment and despite her absences from illness was able to fulfill her educational potential and develop strong social friendships and support groups. Interestingly, I asked no more from the secondary school than I had from the primary school, the difference was I was assured and confident in what I wanted and the staff at the secondary were more open to suggestion and had a desire to support the individual child rather than looking at it as a time consuming inconvenience.

The underlying message is the same one, be strong, be positive and be brave and you can secure the best outcome from the school for your child. Your child can do everything everyone else can with a bit of consideration and support. My lovely girl is now at college taking her 'A' levels, thriving and wanting to go to University. OB does not have to reduce your choices or limit your dreams, you just need the right support.

Chapter 9

Oxygen dependency

For some children with OB life means being attached to an oxygen cylinder 24/7 via cannula or it may be that your child needs to use positive airway pressure devices like CPAP or BiPAP machines. Sometimes they are used just at night or as needed. Even if your child does not need oxygen all the time you will probably have experienced times in hospital or whilst travelling on an airplane when it is required. All this brings with it many challenges for both parent and child. The worry and stress of dealing with a toddler racing around attached to tubing or a child in school with oxygen needs can be overwhelming.

> *CPAP- (Continuous Positive Airway Pressure)-This machine pushes one level of constant air pressure to the patient using a face or nose mask.*
>
> *Bi-PAP - (Bi-Level positive air pressure) -This machine pushes two levels of air pressure again using a face or nose mask. The machine helps push air and oxygen into the lungs and helps to hold the lungs inflated. This machine requires less effort from the patient.*

As with everything else the more knowledge you have the better you can plan and develop a strategy for dealing with the day to day issues. What seems like an insurmountable problem at the start soon becomes just part of everyday life.

Caring for a child receiving oxygen therapy at home is a complex process that requires planning and communication to ensure support and information are available to children and the parents and carers. As the parents and carers you should be involved in discussions as early as possible and on an ongoing basis.

When you have a sick baby it's stressful enough but adding the worry of dealing with oxygen requirements is terrible for many parents. There is the fear that the baby can't tell you what's wrong and it's tempting to be constantly over monitoring every breath. However as with all babies, a stressed parent makes a stressed baby, so the first rule is relax.

Your respiratory paediatrician will have explained and prescribed the amount of oxygen required and you should have received information and a support plan. Make sure you have discussed with your doctor what signals your baby may give which would indicate they need more oxygen.

Using an oxygen saturation monitor, which measures your baby's oxygen level, may give you reassurance, though some doctors do not encourage this, so discuss the idea with your Consultant.

Babies are pretty resilient things actually and they mostly won't know any different so whilst you are consumed with emotion and guilt over the fact that your little one is attached to tubes, they probably neither know nor care much about it.

Make sure that you work on your relationship with your respiratory or oxygen nurse because the better relationships you build the more confident and supported you will feel. If you are ever unsure or just need advice, always ask rather than worrying alone at home. Talking to others who understand is always brilliant and the Breathtakers closed face book page is great forum to share with other parents who understand your worries and concerns.

When your child becomes a toddler, of course your worst nightmares begin, as they are just like any other child and simply want to run around and play. They will at first have no concept that there is the limitation of a length of attached tubing. Here's where you need to get innovative and most parents devise all sorts of strategies for dealing with this. Simple things like making sure the cylinder is secure and doesn't fall over, ensuring the tubing doesn't become a trip hazard or become trapped or blocked, can help. Once you've got a strategy worked out it will all seem so much less daunting. You can still do most things with your toddler with a few adjustments and pre planning, even swimming if your consultant thinks it ok.

Toddlers are now of course aware that they have prongs in their nose and pulling them out on regular basis is great fun for them but not you. Using fun plasters or stickers can distract and even at young age toddlers can understand the necessity of leaving nasal prongs or a mask on if it's explained in the right way. Siblings too soon get used to working around the tubes and children are very accepting generally.

For your child the oxygen and tubes are simply an extension of themselves, they will soon learn how far they can run around on the length of tube and devise lots of little tricks themselves to make it easier.

Sending your toddler to nursery may also seem a huge challenge. Many nurseries will already have a written policy for oxygen dependent children, if not communication with the nursery is the key. Arrange a meeting with the staff to make sure it all runs smoothly. The more they understand about your child's needs the easier it will be. Your oxygen supplier should be able to supply oxygen directly to the nursery and companies like Air Products are very supportive and knowledgeable. Don't forget to let your local fire station and insurance company know that you have oxygen in the house.

Once your child is attending nursery and then school you will begin to experience the reaction of other children and adults to your child. People will stare and although this may be upsetting its worth remembering that people are naturally curious especially if they have never seen an oxygen dependent child before. Children generally are far more accepting and once it's been explained why your child needs help with their breathing most children just take it in their stride. Adults are sometimes more difficult and sending a letter to all the parents in your child's class explaining briefly your situation, or talking to a group of parents can help. I held a couple of awareness assemblies at Kiri's secondary school and by involving the kids and making it fun with balloons etc, it was a great awareness exercise for students and staff. Mostly her peers were concerned and showed a genuine interest. If you are confident about your child then they become confident themselves and can cope much better in these situations. Kiri is now very happy to explain her condition, she is never apologetic, embarrassed or intimidated by it and as a result everyone just simply accepts that that's how things are. She has a very supportive and caring group of friends who are always ready to ensure she is ok and looked after in social situations that might otherwise be tricky. Yet again your child will follow your lead and learn from it, so set a great example.

The great day hopefully of course is when your child finally comes off oxygen and finds a whole new freedom. Be aware though that this can also bring some separation issues for both you and them. You have grown used to the safety blanket of knowing your child is getting help to breathe, many parents find the transition to no oxygen tricky and many say they are unconsciously still looking and checking for tubes for months afterwards. For your child it may be even harder especially if they have been on oxygen for a long time, the tubes have been part of them and it's how they recognize and define themselves, other people begin to treat them differently now and they may not get as much attention. It's worth being aware that there may be a few behavioral issues whilst everyone adjusts to the new freedoms.

Whilst your child is on oxygen generally other people will be supportive and interested and want to help. People may react differently once your child is oxygen free and there are no visible reminders of your child's condition. This is another part of your journey that will bring different experiences and encounters into your life and help both you and your child develop new coping skills and strategies to take forward in other areas of your life and if nothing else it will develop your sense of humour as you untangle the tubing for twentieth time that day! ☺

Chapter 10

Living with OB

I am often asked by parents, how do we explain OB to our children? How much do we tell them and when? How can we help them understand what is happening?

This is an area when as a parent you are probably far more anxious than your child. If they have had OB since being a baby or toddler and they have never known anything different, for them it's quite normal, it's only you making the comparisons and feeling guilty. Children are far more accepting than adults and at this young age they have no real idea of the challenges and restrictions of their illness, all they want to do is have fun, so let them. It's very hard not to transfer our anxieties to our children but it's worth remembering they are first and foremost simply children and the OB is just an added dimension. Children who are happy and have fun stay healthier and are more resilient to infection.

If children are older when they become poorly they may well remember what life was like before the disease and this needs to be handled carefully and they may need professional emotional support. My rule of thumb is tell them what they ask and no more. Children ask very direct and straightforward questions and they generally only ask what they can handle answers too, as adults we often torture ourselves by agonizing over the details. Keep it simple, when they are ready to find out more they will ask. This is not a question of hiding the truth but simply giving your child the appropriate level of information at any given time. I compare it to the sex education talk; the answer you give your four year old as to *'where do babies come from?'* is very different to the one you'd discuss with your fourteen year old. Keep it age appropriate when they want more, they will ask for more but only when they are ready.

Our Consultant still tells the lovely story of Kiri asking him why he simply couldn't shrink himself, travel down inside her lungs and remove the bad stuff to make her better. Pure nine year old logic and a good example that your child is thinking and understanding on very different and much more straightforward level than you are. Though he has still not mastered this technique by the way, he has never forgotten the concept!

Parents also get very anxious about what is discussed at medical appointments in front of their children. In my experience most of it goes over their head at a young age and if they do pick up on something they don't understand they will ask you later just from natural curiosity. If you are really perturbed ask a nurse or take someone with you to the appointment, to take your child out of the room whilst you discuss some things with the consultant. It is very important though that your child is included in discussions as this is a gradual learning experience for them. A good medical professional will always try to include your child in the process; this is very empowering for the child. Remember as young adults they will have to take responsibility for their own health, this may seem a long way in the future if your child is a toddler, but you are their role model and they will naturally take cues from you. The way you behave at medical appointments will be how they will behave in the future. The more controlled, calm and assertive you are then so they will be in the future. You are giving them great coping skills by exhibiting confident and positive behavior. If you end up in tears and angry at every single appointment remember you are simply teaching your child that that is the way to behave in the future. Although it's very hard to always be self controlled at such a scary and emotional time try and keep in mind that your child is like a little sponge soaking up your reactions. As their parent they simply believe everything you say or do is right.

Dealing with the emotional and psychological effects of living with chronic disease is complicated and often unpredictable. This is sadly an area of huge neglect in terms of available support and usually it is only after a crisis has occurred that medical resources can be sought. Please refer to our route map for more information about getting support with mental health issues. http://www.routemap.breathtakers.org.uk/

Whilst we talked about the whole grieving process for you as an adult in a previous chapter, children too need a strong framework of reference and support to help them deal with the challenges they are facing. From personal experience I know that referral to mental health services only usually comes after long and hard persistent struggles and then is only offered as a short term strategy. This 'fighting fires' approach is often not effective long term, is distressing and tends to stick a plaster on the real problems rather than healing the wound underneath. Of course at the root of the lack of these services is inadequate NHS funding but when it's your child in crisis that is little consolation. The message remains the same throughout this book, be strong. Keep pushing for your child because if you don't no-one else will. I believe all children and families should, as matter of course, be offered professional emotional support but in the absence of this ideal there are things you can do ☺

Tips to keeping things in perspective for your child

Anxiety – Even very young children can suffer from anxiety and fear. It manifests itself in many ways from bed wetting, sleepless nights, bad behavior, withdrawal, telling lies, physical violence, eating disorders or in extreme cases self harm or actual physical disorders.

It is much harder for a child to verbalize their fears than an adult, they also may feel guilty and don't want to upset you. Rather like exercising our 'Chimp' as Dr Steve Peters suggests in his book, children to need to let out all that anger, fear and frustration and we can help them do that in a safe way.

Acknowledge the fear- Give your child permission to be angry, sad or frustrated. Tell them it's ok to feel all these things. Crying with your child can be very comforting for them (though not too often!!). Let them know they don't have to be brave all the time and that this illness really isn't fair.

Get creative - Drawing, writing, clay, water and sand play opportunities are all great forms of therapy. For older children poetry, music, sculpting, art and design can channel fears and frustration in a creative and effective way. Be prepared though you may be shocked at the depth of feeling that emerges here but it is all positive and 'better out then in'.

Get motivated- Keeping a diary or an 'inspiration board' can be helpful and a great motivator. Set goals and celebrate achievements with your child. Let them know you are in this thing together, be a team and a strong one.

Put the worries to bed- For us a small set of worry dolls that each night were named, acknowledged and put in a pillow case under the bed succinctly ensured that all those niggling fears had been dealt with and put away each night, encouraging a restful night's sleep. There are lots of variations of this one but anything simple works, it's the act of acknowledging and dealing with each fear that is important here.

Celebrate the unusual- Let your child know that being different is ok and great. Dealing with the reactions of others especially when they are negative is tough for adults let alone children. Social exclusion is a challenge sometimes. I loved the Mum who had a t-shirt printed which said. 'Yes stare, I am beautiful' when she got so fed up of negative reactions when she took her oxygen dependent child out. Don't get defensive, get smart, laugh at the shallowness of others and help your child be confident in who they are. Celebrate the perks, you're always going to be the first to board the plane, if your child needs to use a wheelchair on school trips the other kids will all be fighting to be the one to push them, you can go straight to the front of the queue at the theme park and who else gets to meet the celebs at the end of the show for a signed autograph just because of who they are. There's always an upside ☺

Reward and recognize the milestones- Most children collect achievement certificates for great work at school or sports activities. Your child can do that too of course but *you* can also acknowledge their medical journey, after all this is a huge part of their life. When she was younger each time my daughter had a medical procedure, operation or treatment she got to choose a new glass bead. These were then made into a bracelet (eventually several bracelets). It became quite a discussion point and a way of others acknowledging her journey, how brave she was and how well she was doing. She had great fun choosing pretty beads and could tell you what each one represented; it was almost like a badge of honour. Boys can collect medals or figures or anything really that marks those milestones in a positive way. This is a simple idea but very effective. We found that all my daughters friends wanted a bracelet too but of course couldn't have one and suddenly she was elevated to superstar status amongst her nine and ten year old peers ☺

Recognize and react – You are the one who knows your child best, you will pick up before anyone else that things are going wrong emotionally. Don't wait until it gets to a crisis before you do something. The chances are the problems will not just go away by themselves. By using your skills as a great parent, (which you have and are) and leading by example (which you can do), you can support and nurture your child enabling them to develop fabulous confidence and coping skills. Children with chronic disease are often very mature in many ways simply because they have had to cope with situations that other healthy children have not. The danger is that we expect them to cope emotionally at a much higher level than other children. They are still just children even if they do possess wisdom way beyond their years in many ways.

If all else fails get help – If you recognize that despite all your great efforts things are sliding out of control go and get help for your child. There is sadly still some stigma attached to mental health issues, which I find ridiculous and judgemental. It goes without saying that if your child broke their leg you'd get it fixed so if they have a mental health problem, get it looked at. It is not a reflection on you or your family or even your child. You have been given a very challenging hand to work with and mental health support is just one tool in the box to help you get through it. Great mental health has very positive effects on overall physical health.

The emotional dimensions of chronic conditions such as Obliterative Bronchiolitis are often overlooked when medical care is considered. It can be difficult to diagnose depression in the chronically medically ill but diagnosis and treatment are essential. Often doctors are very well equipped to deal with the biomedical aspects of care but not for the challenges of understanding the psychological, social, and cultural dimensions of illness and health. However doctors can play an important part in helping their patients to maintain healthy coping skills.

Studies have shown mental health challenges lead to a lower quality of life, less ability to function on a day to day level, lessened ability to maintain stable health levels, decreased adherence to therapeutic interventions and worse self management of the disease. The ability for a child or adolescent with OB to cope emotionally depends on multiple factors. These include risk factors related to the illness itself and resistance factors related to the individual.

It has been suggested that the degree to which an illness impairs physical functioning seems to increase the risk of psychological problems, but the relationship is complicated by other factors. For example the visibility of illness may contribute to improved psychological functioning because the inability to hide or deny the condition may compel the child to adjust and accept his status. Often for children with OB who are not oxygen dependent it is frustrating as they appear healthy and others find it difficult to empathise or recognize their challenges and therefore in this case the psychological factors may be increased.

The severity and the course of the illness, and the direct threat to life also influence psychological concerns and outcome. Thus, fear of the unknown or increasing disability may increase over time if the disease progresses or changes.

It is not unusual for children who are hospitalised for long periods of time to develop sleep, eating, or behavioural problems due to constant waking by staff, physical restriction from intravenous lines and unappealing food, and to experience the feeling of frustration and lack of control.

The most common psychological problems and areas to be alert for are:

- **Internalizing problems:** anxiety, depression, fear, hopelessness, helplessness, loss of control, frustration.
- **Externalizing problems:** aggression, noncompliance, withdrawal.

- **Somatic complaints:** pain and impaired functioning.
- **Self-concept issues:** poor self-image, low self-esteem, changed or negative identity.
- **Social and educational difficulties:** academic and learning problems, decreased or deficient social competence.

Things that can help:

Education: The importance of educating both parents and children about a disease like OB or any chronic disease, its cause, course, treatment, and long term effect is often overlooked. Understanding of this information about the disease is influenced by the patient's age, cognitive ability, and psychological style. Children, like adults, vary as to the amount and type of information that is useful. Educating a child and family is not an all-or-nothing, single event. Accurate, honest information must be transmitted in language appropriate to a child's age, when he or she is ready and perhaps repeated at different times and in different formats. This also means not making unrealistic promises such as *'this won't hurt'* for example when clearly a certain medical procedure will hurt in reality.

A long term view of education is also important. Education about appropriate parent-child interactions can decrease parents' overprotective tendencies and the child's adoption of the "sick" role. Illness information and guidance about interacting with the health care system and staff also can empower children and parents to be useful advocates and care partners. These are things you can discuss with your consultant or go to Breathtakers website for more information.

Cognitive-behavioural strategies: This all sounds very scary but working with the appropriate professional can help provide behavioural techniques which can help a child or teen identify the source of stress, change how it is perceived, and teach new behaviours. The goal of this approach is to reduce the impact of the stress and to change feelings and consequent experiences. Cognitive components can include exploration of the link between thoughts and actions and training in more helpful ways of thinking about problems or symptoms.

Play and Art - can also be utilized in conjunction with role play, imagery and relaxation strategies.

Social skills training: Given that problematic peer relationships can impact later on psychosocial development, improving social functioning can have a positive effect.

Family therapy and group work: As there is an interactive relationship between the child's illness and family and friends, working within a larger context can be helpful. Family work can be included in the ongoing management of a chronic illness with life-long duration, such as OB, where the family members can exert a positive effect on illness management. It can also be helpful for ventilation of feelings and clarification of misinformation by children and their siblings.

Take a look at our route map or talk to your doctor about how you can find out more about mental health support. It is a hugely important area and must be addressed sensibly; mental health issues will not simply go away by themselves and if left can quickly get out of control. As with everything else be confident, positive and take control.

Transition to adult services:
When your child is between the ages of sixteen and eighteen years old your consultant will arrange for the transition to adult services, though the transition process can begin many years earlier. Most hospitals have a transitional plan and will work with you to make the whole event smooth for everyone. As with everything else the more information you have the better this process will flow. This can be a worrying time for you and your son or daughter. You have probably been under the care of your respiratory team for many years and feel confident and safe in their care. However it need not be a stressful time if approached calmly and confidently.

This is the part of our journey that we are currently taking in our family and although leaving the safety net of the respiratory team who know us so well seems a bit scary, actually it is just another part of the process. It is also a celebration that your child has become an adult and is now competently and with your support, taking control of their own health decisions. It does not mean that you cannot continue to support them of course but acknowledges their responsibility for their own health and is a positive step towards their future as adults.

Transition should be a gradual process, which gives everyone time to feel prepared and ready to make the move to adult services. Moving to adult health care services brings significant differences in the environment, expectations and culture.

Here are a few things to help.

- Start the process many years before it happens by simply talking about it.
- Gradually allow your child to take over aspects of their own care and routines.
- Ensure they know what drugs they take, how much and how often.
- Encourage them to ask questions about their condition and treatments.
- Make sure they understand the common medical terms associated with their condition.
- Encourage them to stay in hospital without you.
- Encourage them to talk to their consultant rather than you doing it or to see them alone at least for part of the consultation.
- Let them keep track of appointments.

- Acknowledge that saying goodbye to the paediatric team is sad but necessary. Let them say goodbye.
- Arrange a visit to the new clinic and meet the new team. Most consultants will arrange a joint hand over appointment with the new consultant.

Celebrate the milestone; your own approach to this will have a big influence and enable your child to be confident and assertive in the future as they manage their own health care. You are giving them great gifts of independence and self belief in their own competence.

Chapter 11

Your stories

One of the main objectives of Breathtakers OB Trust has been to facilitate contact between families, enabling them to grow by supporting each other. I have had the absolute privilege to get to know many families and travel their journey so far with them, learning more and more as I go. Our stories are emotive and powerful and the more we tell them the more support and awareness we encourage. So I ask you all too just tell your story often and everywhere and let the world know about OB so that in the future no family will feel alone in this strange journey.

So far I have talked about OB from the perspective of my own experiences, the OB Trust or as a parent but what if you are the one with the disease?

What is life like on a day to day basis for you? If you have had this disease since you were a baby or very small child then it probably just seems normal, after all you have never known anything different neither do you have anything to compare it with. If you remember what life was like before OB then coming to terms with it may have been challenging especially if you have not had any emotional or psychological support. I recall one OB teenager telling me she actually feared getting better, as she had always had OB and that was what she knew and she loved her life just as it was.

So here is the perspective of OB from some of our fabulous families, OB children and young adults

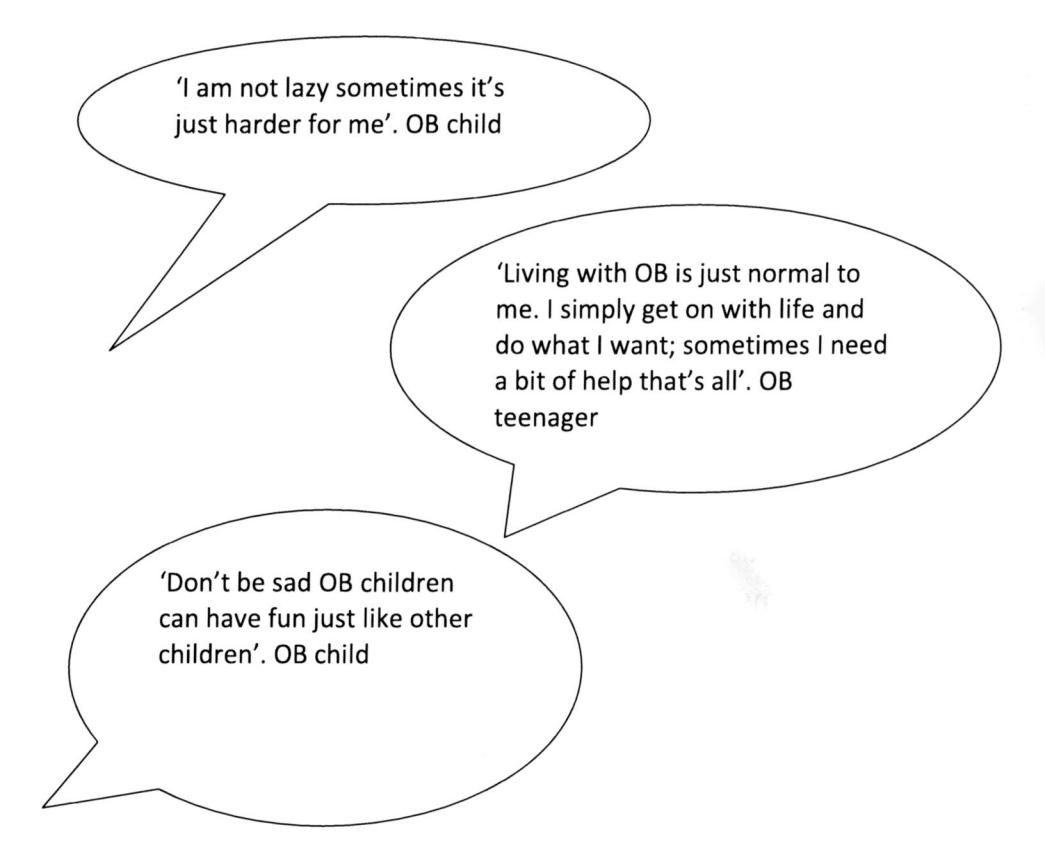

'I am not lazy sometimes it's just harder for me'. OB child

'Living with OB is just normal to me. I simply get on with life and do what I want; sometimes I need a bit of help that's all'. OB teenager

'Don't be sad OB children can have fun just like other children'. OB child

William Edward Phin

William was born in December 2009 as a 'normal' healthy baby. He managed to get through his first year without any health problems, and rarely even had a cold. Just after Christmas he got sick with flu like symptoms and when he did not get over this, he was admitted to hospital. After two weeks in hospital with suspected pneumonia William began to show signs of recovery and we were allowed to bring him home. The prognosis was that William would gradually recover and would return to full health. At the time we had no idea it would be eighteen months before we would be able to take another picture of our son without a nasal cannula.

Within a week we were back in hospital again. This time the atmosphere felt different. William was showing little sign of improvement and we didn't have a clear diagnosis to explain why he was so poorly. On the 26th January we were transferred into the care of the pediatric respiratory team at the Great North Children's hospital in Newcastle. The team were fantastic. Although they could not give us an immediate diagnosis, they were able to stabilize William and on 4th February, 2011 we returned home.

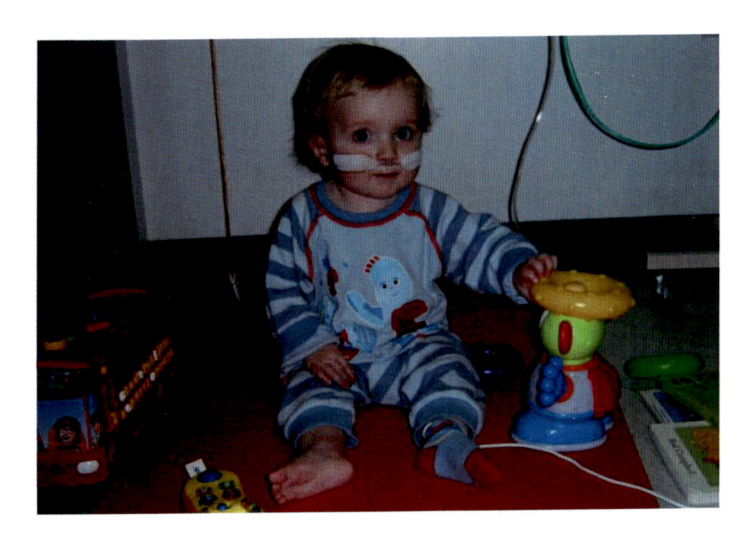

Taking William home with oxygen was quite a daunting experience. We spent the first couple of weeks constantly checking the supply: did we have enough oxygen? When would it run out? When do we need to reorder? Every trip out involved detailed logistical planning: where are we going? How long will it take? How long will the oxygen last? Those first couple of weeks were difficult but as we became more accustomed to having a child on oxygen we began to feel more relaxed.

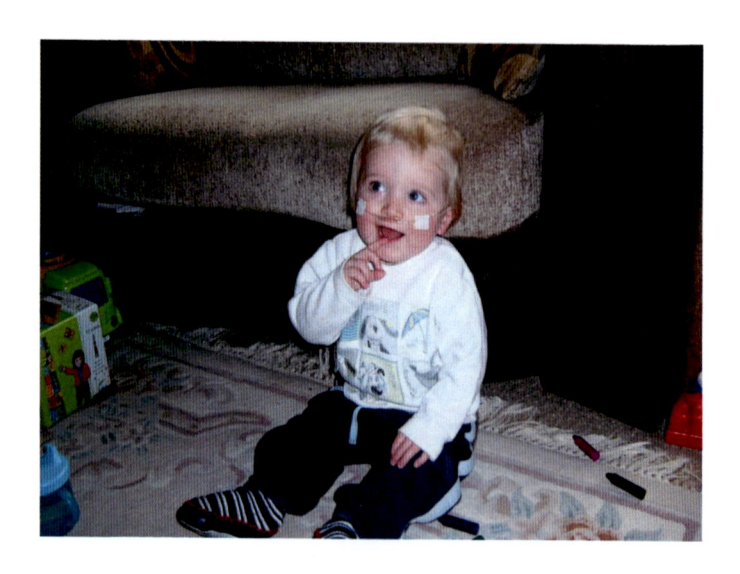

William had a CT scan on March 10th 2011 where we finally received the diagnosis that he had Obliterative

Bronchiolitis and post infectious bronchiectasis. We knew that this was the most likely diagnosis; however, it still came as a blow to get confirmation that our little boy had a debilitating illness. The prognosis looked bleak: potentially a lifetime on oxygen therapy, physiotherapy, prophylactic antibiotics a high probability of frequent hospitalization. Although the diagnosis was devastating there was also a sense of relief to finally have a definitive diagnosis and a clear plan of action to support William and manage the condition.

The next big challenge we faced was in May 2011 when it was suggested that we try William with non invasive ventilation. The treatment would take over William's breathing while he slept and help force air deeper into the airways than he could normally achieve with his own breathing.

After a few failed attempts we successfully got the mask on William and he went through a full night wearing his mask. This was the first time the medical team had heard of a child of William's age tolerating the treatment for so long so quickly after it had been introduced

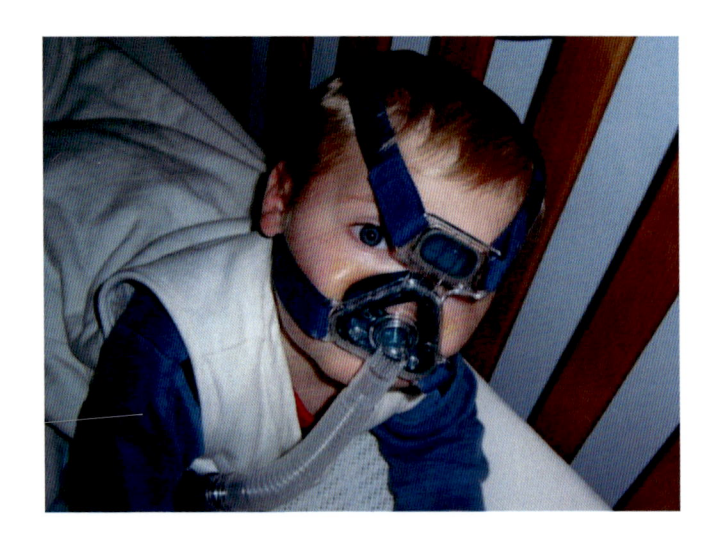

William on Nippy: 14th June 2011.

Life took on a semblance of normality. Morning physiotherapy, antibiotics, trips out with oxygen in tow, evening physiotherapy, more antibiotics, nippy mask and bed. William was now fully mobile and we were becoming more adept at negotiating climbing frames and participating in other childhood escapades with four feet of tubing tethering us to a highly inquisitive and active child.

The regular check-ups with the respiratory team continued. With every visit we were told how well William was progressing but there was never a timescale on when or if we would be able to stop the oxygen therapy. The good news was that the doctors were supportive of us trying to slowly reduce William's oxygen levels to see how he coped.

In April 2012 we returned to hospital to see if William could maintain his oxygen saturation levels as his oxygen therapy was reduced. The following morning William was no longer on his oxygen therapy and was showing no adverse affects. After a challenging and tumultuous year we were able to take William home without an oxygen cylinder in tow. It was like a huge weight had been lifted and we now had a greater sense of freedom to live like "normal" families do. For the first couple of weeks William still asked one of us to follow him around. He must have assumed that we had to follow him whenever he went anywhere. However, over time he grew in confidence and barely remembers his time on oxygen therapy. We were also able to stop the night time ventilation and in time all of the tubing, compressors and oxygen cylinders were removed from the house.

The new sense of freedom allowed us to take a day trip to York on the train and in July 2012 we went on our first family holiday to the Lake District.

We still perform physiotherapy twice a day, administer prophylactic antibiotics, attend clinic for check-ups and have an increased level of vigilance at the first sign of a cough or cold. Although there is no known cure for the condition we manage the symptoms and don't let the condition dictate how we live our lives. Having witnessed William's rapid decline in health and subsequent improvement, we have a greater understanding of what is important to us and what sacrifices we would be willing to make to give William the best opportunities to live his life to the full.

We were lucky when we got the diagnosis of Obliterative Bronchiolitis that the consultant made us aware of a charity called Breathtakers. After the initial shock of the diagnosis calmed down a little, we got in touch with Lynne for help and support. Although having a child with OB can be quite lonely at times (when you are avoiding friends and family because they have colds, viruses, flu etc that you don't want to risk getting infected with), the Breathtakers community makes you feel very welcome. It can sometimes be hard to ask your consultant questions for fear of feeling silly, but you don't have to feel that way with anyone who is involved with Breathtakers. Everyone is great at providing support, sharing their own stories and offering advice where they can. Due to this support, we have tried to do all we can to help support the charity. We have raised money by doing a zip slide from the Tyne Bridge Newcastle. We managed to convince some of our friends to run the Great North Run half marathon. One of our friends ran the London Marathon for Breathtakers. William's Dad and Uncle Bryn are going to undertake a 10K obstacle course challenge at the end of July to raise more money.

Thanks

Fiona and Duncan Phin

Laylun Leio Nason

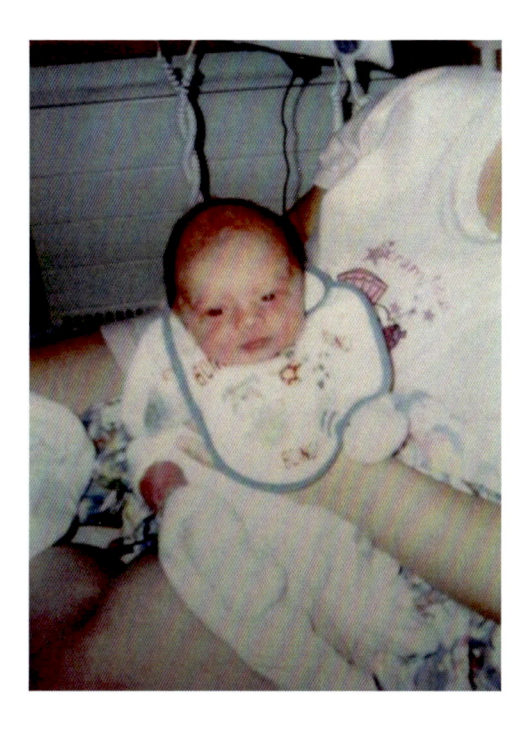

Laylun Leio Nason was born on the 12th November 2005, after a normal pregnancy but rather fast labour of thirty-seven minutes. He weighed in at 6lbs 13ozs and immediately needed IV's for Strep B. At twenty-three days old he developed pneumonia which resulted in seven more weeks in hospital, followed by two weeks at home and then another nine weeks in hospital with pneumonia and RSV. Not a great start for him. Respiratory syncytial virus (RSV) is a major cause of respiratory illness in young children. For the next twenty-three months Laylun spent the majority of his young life in hospital spending only sixteen weeks at home during that time. He was now oxygen dependant and at four months old was diagnosed as 'failure to thrive'; and at six months after steroid treatment as a 'fat happy wheezer'. What followed were several more episodes of turning blue, stopping breathing and bouts of RSV.

In January 2007 Laylun contracted chicken pox and was readmitted to hospital on the 2nd of February where he remained for the next eight months. During this time he spent some time in the PICU on a Bi-PAP machine and was tested for immune deficiencies, cystic fibrosis and PCD (Primary Ciliary Dyskinesia). He had lumbar punctures for meningitis but initially we were no clearer as to a diagnosis.

This was an extremely stressful time for the whole family, not helped by not being able to find any support and feeling ' not believed' by medical staff. At one stage we seemed to have every kind of paediatric consultant known to man standing around his bed, none of whom knew what was wrong. We were told several times to bring the family to say goodbye to Laylun as they could not do anything else for him. I refused to do this though as I knew he was such a fighter and it would be like giving up on him.

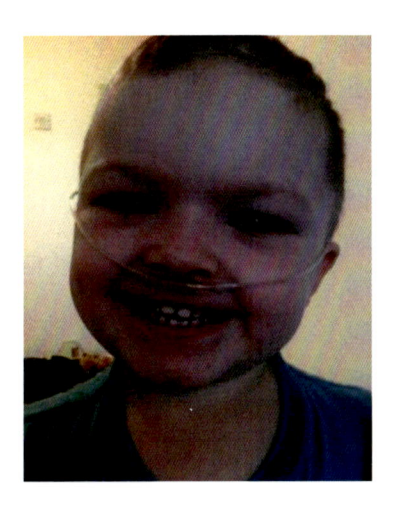

In April 2007 we first met our brilliant respiratory consultant at Queen Mary's Nottingham, without whom we are not sure where we would be. He took one look at Laylun and said 'I think he has OB, I've seen it before'. He immediately started Laylun on Azithromycin, steroids, physiotherapy and did CT scans. These showed the mosaic patterns typical of OB. At last we had a diagnosis but could not find out anything about the condition or any help or support.

Eventually we took Laylun home on oxygen which was terrifying at first but it soon became the 'norm'. We learned to stop panicking every time he twisted the tube or pulled out the prongs and let him work his own ways out of dealing with it all. He soon learned to race around the house and the tubes just became an extension of himself. Though he never did work out when playing hide and seek how he could be found so quickly by his siblings who just followed the trail of tubes☺. I know it's very daunting for parents to have a toddler on oxygen but it does get easier with time and you learn little tricks to help you, like putting the tube down the inside of the back of their clothing to stop it twisting. It is important not to let worrying over oxygen take over everything else or you miss all the fun.

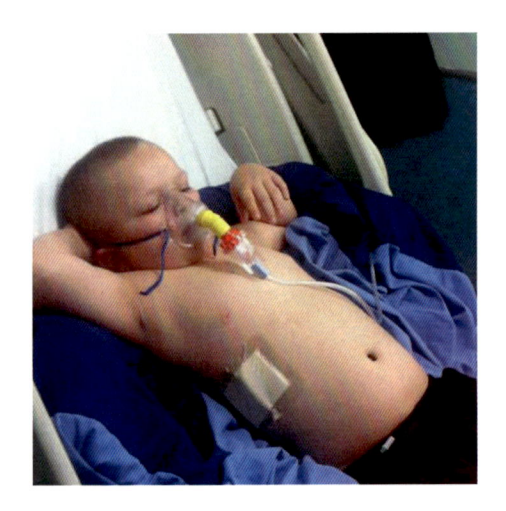

Going to nursery and school can also seem like a huge hurdle. We wanted Laylun to be able to experience a normal life and mix with other children but there was a lot of fear about infection and how other children and adults would react to him being on oxygen, would he begin to feel 'different'? The key is communication and education. Making sure you involve the staff, community nurse, SENCO, children and other parents so that everybody is aware of your child's condition and knows what to do if things do go wrong. Children are very accepting and Laylun's friends are very protective of him.

In August 2011 Laylun finally came off oxygen; this was both an exciting and scary time for us. Although it was brilliant to see Laylun finally free from all those tubes they were a kind of safety net and for a long time afterwards we were still thinking he was attached to them and looking to move them or check them. For Laylun this has also been a time of adjustment and there have been some separation issues for him, after all they have always been part of him and brought him attention and comfort. Though he loves the freedom to rush around unhindered of course and just be a boy.

No longer being on oxygen also alters other peoples' perceptions of his condition too and sometimes it needs a gentle reminder that just because he 'looks well' he is not completely better. He now has a PortaCath fitted so that he can have his IV's regularly and he has adapted to this well and as bravely as ever.

Throughout this journey I have struggled sometimes to cope with it all and have been overwhelmed. Trying to look after our other 3 children and Laylun has been hard and sometimes lonely. Finding Breathtakers really helped me to turn a corner, grow stronger and more determined. I do believe that there have been many good things that have come from this journey. I now appreciate how precious life is and I don't take anything for granted, we have become a stronger family and I am a very different person (for the better).

I believe there are reasons that this has happened even though it is unfair that Laylun should have OB. For example I always encourage the medical students at the hospital to learn about Laylun and then hopefully no other family will have to go through the things we have when doctors do not know what OB is.

I have met some amazing people and established great friendships with people who really understand what we have gone through and we can support each other. Laylun made a very special friend in hospital called Connor. Connor, aged 8, has now sadly passed away from leukemia but the friendship and bond with his mother continues and we now produce bags called 'Connor and Laylun comfort packs' which we give to the hospital. These are emergency packs for Mums who have to stay in hospital with their children unexpectedly and contain things like toothpaste/shampoo/£1 for the phone etc and always a motivational message, because we know just what to feels like to suddenly be admitted to a ward and have nothing with you. It's a small way for us to give back and help others and another positive thing to have come from all this.

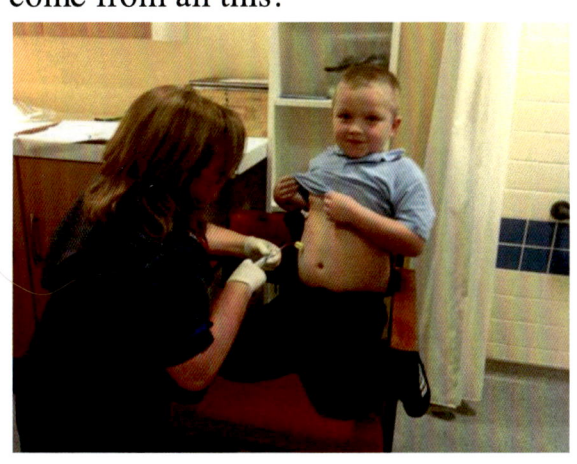

I have also seen the amazing generosity and kindness of people who give up their time and money to help. One lovely lady arranged a winter wonderland visit in her garden for Laylun because he was unable to go on a wish day to Lapland whilst he was on oxygen. This has now been continued each year and many poorly children have been able to enjoy this wonderful experience, another extraordinary and wonderful thing to have come from this journey.

Laylun's story has been a hard one and at the start did seem very bleak but he is now a happy cheeky boy full of fun and enjoying every day and I hope this is an inspiration for others to see.

My lovely family

By Gemma Nason

Harry Blow

I was born twelve weeks and six days early weighing in at just over 2lbs. I spent my first five months in hospital where I was ventilated for over six weeks. When I left hospital I still only weighed 7 lbs! In my first year of life I was hospitalized many times for various chest infections culminating in an adenovirus infection at twenty months old, which left me needing oxygen when I slept. According to Mum it was touch and go many times and I gave them many sleepless nights. When I was four I contracted the adenovirus again, how unlucky was that, I was in hospital for three months and left needing oxygen all the time with the diagnosis of OB. Docs were concerned that I was steadily getting worse so was put on the transplant list for a heart and lung transplant.

No donor was ever found and luckily by the time I was six my health had stopped deteriorating and I was taken off the list even though I still required supplementary oxygen all the time.

From six-sixteen years of age I attended main stream school most of the time. I had quite a lot of time off due to chest infections and general tiredness. I had a portable oxygen system that Mum and Dad had found in America which enabled me to become more mobile and independent. I always had a one to one helper at school but was able to join in most activities including sport and extra-curricular stuff. I even went on an outward bound trip with school with my big brother as my helper!

I left school at sixteen with five GCSE's then did various courses at local colleges. Again I missed some lessons due to being tired but luckily have suffered very few chest infections since about the age of thirteen or fourteen. I've not been in hospital since I was ten - touch wood. I have travelled to various countries with my parents, sometimes very difficult for Mum to organize oxygen and health insurance but have been to Barbados, America, Egypt and lots of places in Europe - lucky me.

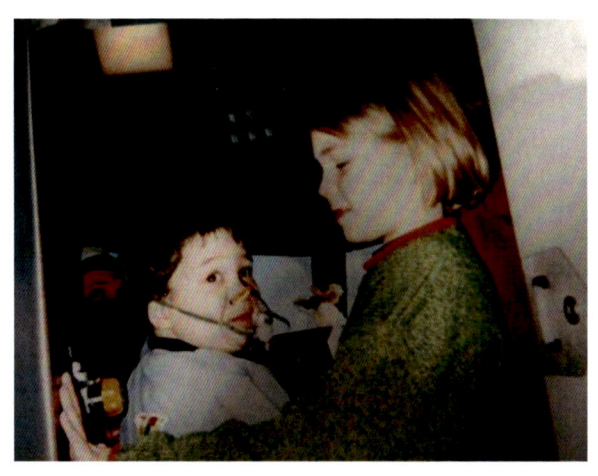

I had a great time for six months last year when I did some work experience at a film production company in London, where I got to experience life living away from home (I rented the sofa at my sister's flat!) which shows that even with my condition I can live an independent life it was finances that cut my time in London short not my health! I enjoy going to music festivals, organizing the oxygen was always a bit of a pain but I now have a portable concentrator which has made my life much easier. Just spent a fantastic five days this year at the Glastonbury festival. One positive to come out of being registered disabled is an extra free ticket for the festival, better camping facilities and better loos!!

I now have a great permanent job as a carer in the community. I manage to work about twenty-five hours per week, but do get very tired and have to lay low sometimes on my days off to ensure I have enough energy to party! All in all OB has thrown up many challenges most of which I've been able to overcome, but it has made me who I am today. Here's me at Glastonbury modeling my portable concentrator!!

Harry ☺

Kiri Thompson

Until I was seven years old I lived in New Zealand. It was fantastic growing up in a different country and climate and experiencing all those different cultures. I was just like any other kid, having fun. I loved swimming and was at my happiest in the water, sea or pool (still am).

Then in 2004 we moved back to England to be near family and friends. As you know from the start of this book I very quickly ended up with OB. I don't want to focus on what happened and what I've lost but instead on what I've gained.

Here's how I see it. I have gained a unique view of the world and anyone who has been seriously ill or has a chronic condition will know what I am talking about. It's an appreciation of life that drives us to do wonderful things and to see the good in everything. In a way I think it is a magical gift that everyone has the potential to have but very few people are privileged to have or to even see it and take advantage of.

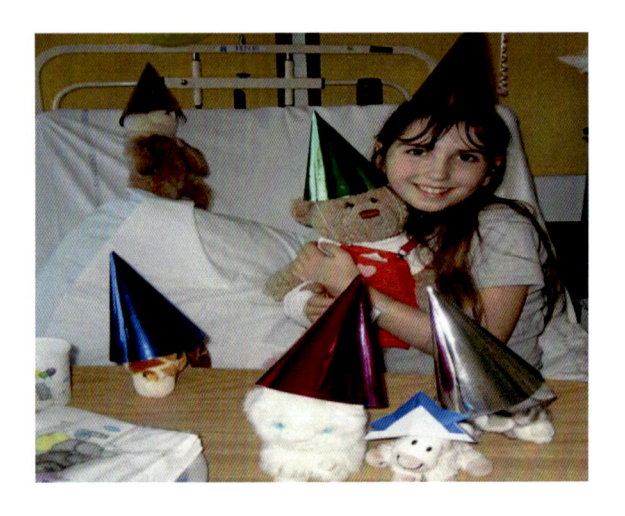

People may say that's looking through rose coloured glasses and is a bad thing but I would completely disagree, it's not about losing reality it's about changing and adapting the reality to your advantage.

So when facing challenges through health, school, travelling and social activities I 'choose' not to do something rather than letting OB dictate that I can't and then I simply 'choose' to do something else. That way you are in control, you choose what you want to do and you turn those choices into your passions. I have a great life; I've travelled to lots of countries and have brilliant friends. So I think my message to everyone is simple, never feel upset, sad or sympathy for me, if anything be a bit envious of the magical gift I have that enables me to make my life wonderful and limitless.

Dream and be happy - Kiri ☺

Many thanks to Harry Blow, Kiri Thompson, Fiona and Duncan Phin, Darren and Gemma Nason who have contributed and shared their stories in this book too ☺

Chapter 12

The extraordinary gifts

Anything is possible. Nine years ago my life could be described as 'normal'. I was pretty much like most other people I guess just getting on with everyday life. I felt I was blessed, after all I had a lovely family and friends, a nice home, travelled on holidays and had an interesting though fairly ordinary job. I didn't think too much about the distant future, I just and went through motions of life every day.

Then the extraordinary and unwanted gift arrived. It turned out to be not just one gift but many, arriving in never ending waves and often disguised initially as problems. The first ones were all terrifying challenges that sometimes seemed insurmountable and brought only sorrow and despair but slowly they were followed by hopeful ones, interesting ones, inspiring ones and amazing ones. They came in many guises, inanimate and animate forms, some stayed, some only visited briefly but they slowly changed my life and the lives of those around me forever.

If anyone had told me back then I would create a charity that supports families all across the world, design and build online resources, train in reflexology, train and become a life, business and charity coach, build a successful business, host national conferences, speak at events and even write another book I would have said they were crazy because I knew nothing about any of those things. Without those extraordinary unwanted gifts that invaded my life I never would have.

My life is defined and brighter now and I don't miss the tiniest detail. I enjoy the moments and never waste them by simply letting the little things slip by unnoticed. I don't spend time on the 'what if's' of life because they are out of my control instead concentrating on the 'now' and making the most of all of it. Even though there have been sorrows and emotional casualties in my journey, they too have brought new understandings and opportunities.

I am a believer of the law of attraction which says that whatever you think about most becomes you're reality. Books like *The Secret, The Magic,* and motivational leaders like Brain Tracy all talk about having gratitude for everything you have, simply saying thank you every day for all the good things in your life. Once you start listing the good things (which are endless) you're brain stops thinking about the bad things, as it can't hold two thoughts at the same time. I practice this all the time and it really works.

Throughout this journey I have steadfastly and some would say stubbornly, held on to my positive beliefs that things could only get better. That whatever terrible things happened, something good would come from it and no matter how bad it seemed for us someone was experiencing something worse. I also passionately believe that just because I couldn't make this all go away for us I could do something very empowering for others, something positive that would help them use the extraordinary gift in a beneficial way in their lives too.

As parents our first instinct is naturally to protect our children from harm. On this particular journey threats come in many forms, a disease that you can't make go away, the fear and pain associated with illness, invasive treatments you can't prevent, disappointments you can't avoid, social relationships you can't make for your children, the unknown future. But there is so much that is in your control, so much you can influence and achieve. If we just turn this whole experience on its head and grab the opportunities to grow and become something very special instead, we can help our children become the superstars we already know they are.

None of us have chosen to be on this journey, none of us want this for our children but we do have a clear choice to either stumble on every stone along the path counting the blisters or to smile and stride out with confidence collecting the gifts on the way and using them to both enhance our armory and give us tools and fuel to keep moving forward.

The future

None of us knows what our future will bring or hold, some of us try to plan for it laying down some contingency plans to buffer ourselves against adversity but none of us really know what is around the next corner. This becomes more complex when a disease like OB becomes part of your world because you have nothing to compare it to, you can't look back and find solutions to help you. It is almost like playing it by ear every day. But what you do have are two clear choices, you can be in control of OB or you can let it control you. I have been privileged to meet some amazing and inspiring people who live with this disease every day. They have made the decision to get on with life and not be defined by their condition; rather they draw strength and courage from their experiences and use that to constantly move forward in a positive and exciting way. Being extraordinary is a gift which brings the ability to embrace life in ways most of us cannot imagine, when living itself transcends the everyday existence most people experience, you are transported to a life truly fulfilled and wonderful. Just getting by and surviving is never enough when you have glimpsed the opportunities offered by the gifts that rarity brings.

Breathtakers OB Trust exists both because of and for, all the OB sufferers and their families across the world. My wish is that it will continue to stand strong and grow, reaching out to more and more families and doctors, raising awareness and offering vital support. I hope my own contribution and involvement will continue as long as the Trust needs me but that ultimately the foundations I have built will enable the charity to stand independently and thrive in the future with new families stepping forward to carry it onward using their gifts, ideas and innovations along the way. Already the extraordinary gifts that have come our way have enabled families to be connected, information to be shared and hope to be ignited. The Trust has been able to provide reliable information, hospital gifts, wish days, respite breaks, educational equipment, medical equipment and research. We have held the first ever OB conference and are now going onto to our second and published our unique Route Map. More doctors and medical professionals are aware of OB than ever before and worldwide OB sufferers have a place that is just for them to share experiences and receive support from. Better still all those are gifts that can shared with more OB families in the future to make their journey easier.

The extraordinary people

Before my OB journey I believe I was blindfolded to many things in life. There were some ups, some downs, but overall I was pretty blinkered to the extraordinary. Then it was if my eyes had suddenly been opened and my senses were assaulted by a whole new level of emotions. They were not all good, some deep despair, soul destroying sadness and paralyzing fear but with that also came incredible compassion, awe inspiring strength and powerful positivity.

My beautiful daughter even as little girl, displayed more strength, bravery and courage than I'd ever seen before and still does and this has inspired me continually on this strange journey. My two wonderful sons have both in different ways shown compassion, strength and courage that I can only be amazed and proud of. Kiri's Dad, family and friends, have all risen to the challenges and often gone way beyond whatever could have been expected of them. The amazing team of people who have helped Breathtakers grow with their constant and unfaltering belief and enthusiasm still move me with their loyalty and dedication.

Our brilliant respiratory consultant and the rest of the respiratory team who have never let us fall over the years. Our trust in you has been unshakeable and proved beyond all doubt.

All the amazing OB families, who have so honestly and openly shared their stories, triumphs, joys and fears with me. I have been privileged to be part of your lives and be part of your own journey to the extraordinary.

Of course if we could simply wave a magic wand we would all wish that we had not been taken on this journey. However it *is* an extraordinary gift that opens your life to amazing people, breathtaking generosity, selfless kindness and empowers you find courage, strength and tenacity that you never thought you had. It makes you appreciate every minute of every day and to never to waste a moment worrying over the 'small stuff'. It brings heights and depths of emotion that you may never have experienced before which although they may bring sorrow also bring an insight and understanding that others have not been privileged to experience. As a person you become wiser, more tolerant and gain a new empathy and understanding of life. It's a rollercoaster journey to the land of the extraordinary and once you arrive you realise that you are extraordinary too.

Lynne

Soaring no limits ☺

©14/08/2013 copyright L Thompson